Final Week dec 19 7.35

act — 11, 12, 14 945
1135

QUESTIONS on chapt 5
6
8
9
10

Principles of Business Computer Programming

DAVID BRECKNER / PETER ABEL
British Columbia Institute of Technology

PRENTICE-HALL, INC., Englewood Cliffs, New Jersey

13-706614-7

Library of Congress Catalog Card No.: 70-123871

Current printing (last digit):

10 9 8 7 6 5 4 3 2

PRENTICE-HALL INTERNATIONAL, INC., London
PRENTICE-HALL OF AUSTRALIA, PTY. LTD., Sydney
PRENTICE-HALL OF CANADA, LTD., Toronto
PRENTICE-HALL OF INDIA PRIVATE LIMITED, New Delhi
PRENTICE-HALL OF JAPAN, INC., Tokyo

Preface

This book presents material covered in the first year of a two-year program of training for computer programmer-analysts at the British Columbia Institute of Technology. However, it does not give instruction in the particular coding languages used in this course for the reasons given later.

Furthermore, the material is presented in a logically developed sequence and only as required to enable the student to tackle the problem at hand. It is not, therefore, an encyclopedic reference-type text. Nor is it intended as a survey-type text for students not interested in becoming professional programmers.

The usual approach of books on this subject has been to present a vast quantity of information either about data processing in general or about a specific computer language. Little or no effort is made to instruct the reader on how he may go about tackling a typical, real-life business program. Further, many of the common types of problems almost invariably encountered in a business environment are often omitted.

The writing of a program can be divided into two main areas: analysis and coding.

In the first, the problem is analyzed and the logical sequence of steps in the solution is decided upon. Usually a flowchart is the result.

In the second stage, the steps shown in the flowchart or other form of solution must be coded into the particular language for the particular computer being used.

It is the first stage, analysis, which is not adequately treated by the existing literature and which we deal with in this text.

This book is unusual in that it does not specify a particular language or a particular computer. For purely illustrative purposes, however, a self-explanatory language is used. Information on actual instruction sets and on computer characteristics is available in many other texts as well as in manufacturers' manuals. It is not the purpose of this book to repeat what is easily available elsewhere. Indeed, the coding of a program is perhaps one of the least difficult steps in programming. What is difficult is the initial *program analysis,* which is *independent* of a specific language.

It has been our experience as professional programmers that certain types of programs recur in various guises in business. Program analysis can be greatly facilitated by recognizing the problem and by applying a generalized solution. Of course, no two programs are identical. But many have important similarities in their logical structure.

As teachers of programming, it has also been our experience that the novice programmer will learn better by programming as soon as possible. However, he is prone to fall into many pitfalls and errors, many of which may be avoided by properly developed training.

This book, therefore, takes a very practical, language-independent, step-by-step approach to the writing of commercial programs.

The reader should use this book in conjunction with manuals on the specific language and the specific computer in which he is interested. The book is recommended for individuals who want to learn the basics of programming, for firms that train their own staff, and for institutions that teach courses in programming. In these cases it is essential that all the problems specified as mandatory be completely programmed and documented to the standards specified. This is important because the only way to become a programmer is to practise writing programs and *getting them to work.*

The book may also be used by those wishing to obtain an understanding of programming techniques without necessarily becoming expert programmers. They may not wish to code all the programming exercises completely, but they should at least prepare all the flowcharts.

D. B.
P. A.

Contents

1

Introduction

PURPOSE OF THIS TEXT

There are many textbooks on the subject of computer programming that cover many different computers (real and imaginary) and many different languages. In general, these texts concentrate on *coding,* i.e., the writing of a set of instructions in a form that the computer can understand and execute. We contend that the most important part of computer programming is not the coding but the designing of the procedure, usually in the form of a *flowchart,* required to solve the problem at hand.

This task requires a sound understanding of business principles, the precise definition of the data to be supplied to the computing system, and a clear specification of the nature and format of the output to be returned by the system. A knowledge of the capabilities of the computer available will then enable a logical procedure to be established which can be translated into an effective computer program.

The establishment of the logical procedure, or flowchart, is the difficult part; the rest is mainly mechanical and routine. There are, however, a number of standard types of procedure which are used over and over again in a variety of business situations. A knowledge of these procedures, with the ability to recognize those situations in which they can be applied, will make the task of flowchart design much less onerous. The following pages cover some of these techniques, set forth in a logically developing sequence for the benefit of the student with no prior experience who is training as a programmer.

HOW TO USE THE TEXT MATERIAL

This text is not written for any particular computer or any particular language. It is a text on principles and techniques applicable to any environment. However, if it is to be used as part of the training of programmers, it is *essential* that the examples be studied and the exercises be actually solved on a *real computer.* The *only* way to *learn* programming is to *write* programs and *get them to work.* It will be necessary, therefore, to have access to a computer and to have a means of learning the language of that computer.

The authors have used the material in this text in the teaching of programming in 1620 S.P.S., 360 Assembler, Fortran II, Fortran IV, PL/I, and Cobol. A student studying any of these or the other common languages will have no difficulty in following the illustrative coding in the text, which might be called PLC (plain language compiler).

FUNDAMENTALS

What Is a Computer?

A computer is a system into which we can feed information, which will perform calculations and manipulations on that information, and which will then return to us the results of the operations in a desirable form. For instance, we might enter information about an employee's hours of work and rate of pay and receive a statement of his gross pay.

We see, then, that there are five basic elements in a computer:

1. Means of feeding information in	INPUT
2. Means for getting answers out	OUTPUT
3. Means for performing calculations	ARITHMETIC OR LOGIC
4. Means for storing values during the processing	STORAGE OR MEMORY
5. Means for controlling operations	CONTROL

Input

The Punched Card. In this text we shall be dealing with the punched card only as a means of feeding information into the computer. The standard Hollerith punched card is shown in Figure 1-1. It measures $3\frac{1}{4} \times 7\frac{3}{8}$ in. and is divided into 80 vertical columns numbered 1-80 and 12 horizontal rows only 10 of which (the lower ones) are marked and numbered 0-9.

The perforation of the card by a rectangular hole at the point where a particular number is printed is used to indicate a value of that number for that particular column. Figure 1-1 shows a value of 7 punched in column 1. Thus we can represent up to 80 digits, each of value 0-9, on one card.

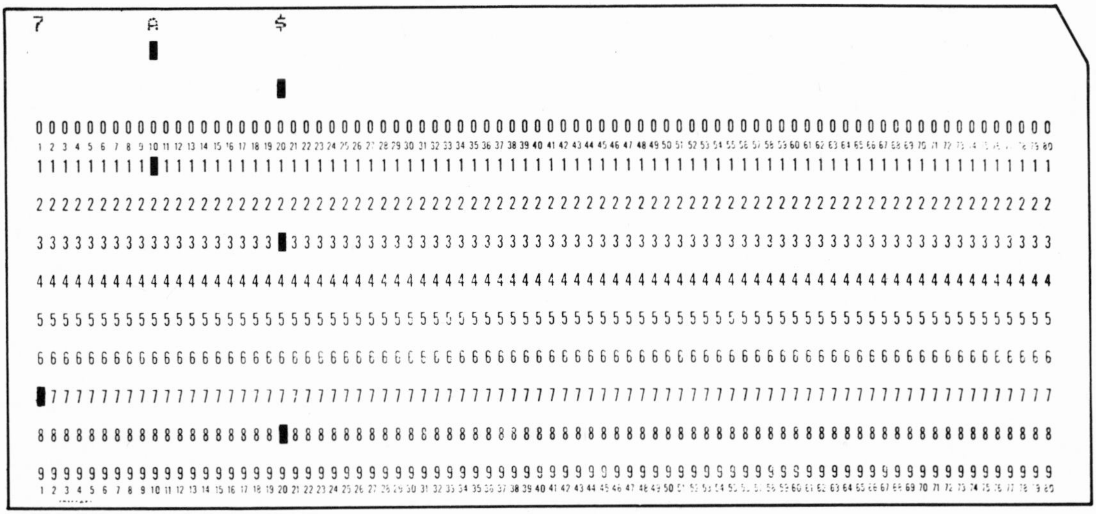

Fig. 1-1.

To represent letters A through Z we use in addition the two unmarked rows at the top of the card. The top one is called the 12 row and the next row, just above the 0 row, is the 11 row. A letter is represented by a combination of a numeric punch 1 to 9 with a punch in one of the top three rows 12, 11, or 0—both punches being in one column. This is called a multipunch. Thus, an A is represented by a combination of a 12 punch and a 1 punch, and a Z by a 0 punch and a 9 punch.

Special characters are also represented by a combination of punches in one column. Thus, a 12 punch alone represents an ampersand (&), and 0 and 1 punch combination represents a slash (/), while a 11, 3, 8 multipunch represents a dollar sign ($).

In this way we can represent up to 80 letters or special characters or any combination of them with numeric digits on one card.

Figure 1-1 shows the letter A in column 10 and the character $ in column 20. Figure 1-2 shows the punching of all the commonly used characters.

The 11 punch alone, sometimes called the X punch, represents the hyphen; it is also normally used to signify a minus sign. Notice that the character punched in each column may also be printed in that column at the top of the card above the 12 row. This is often done purely to facilitate reading of the card by the human operator.

Fields. In most applications of numbers or letters we are not concerned with single characters. We have *numbers* consisting of

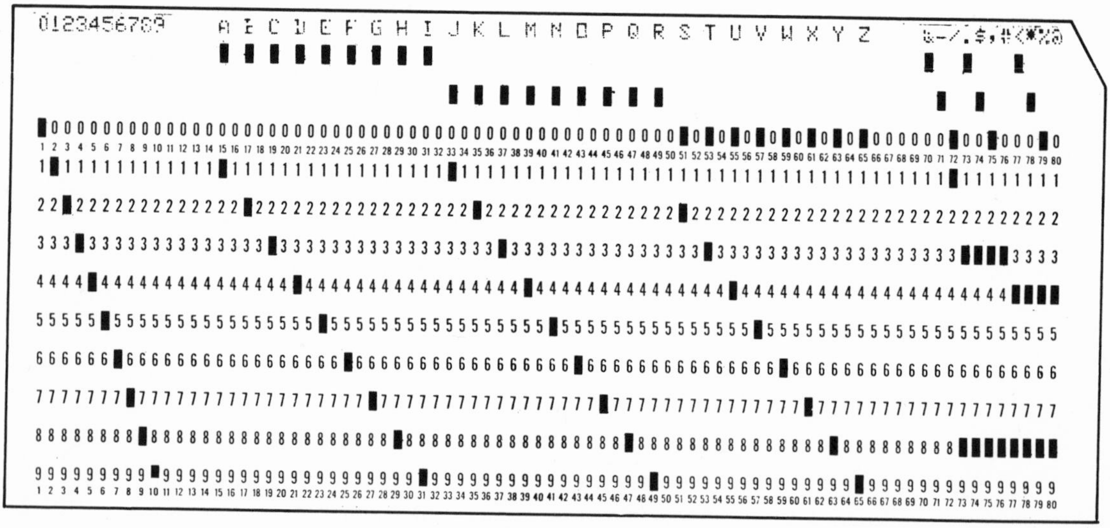

Fig. 1-2.

several digits, e.g., 127, and *words* consisting of several letters, e.g., JANUARY. We may also have combinations of letters and numbers such as in part J273. Such groups of characters would be punched in adjacent columns on the card and form a "field."

A field may be defined as one or more adjacent columns on a card used to record one particular piece of information.

A card will usually contain several fields, each recording a piece of information about some event. For instance a sales card might have "customer number," "name," "date," and "value of goods sold" fields. Each field is composed of several characters punched in a group of adjacent columns and represents one item of information about a business transaction. Such a card is often called a "unit record."

> *Note:* Usually, in punching numbers containing decimal fractions, e.g., dollars and cents, the decimal point is not punched, but its location is understood by definition of the card design.

Also, in punching an amount which requires fewer columns than are provided for that field, the number is right-justified and filled out to the left with zeros, e.g., a five-column field containing the number 269 would be punched 00269.

Alphabetic fields, such as names, are usually left-justified and filled out to the right with blanks, e.g., a nine-column field containing the word APRIL would be punched APRILƀƀƀƀ. The symbol ƀ is used to signify a blank position.

Entry into the Computer. The card is fed mechanically into a card reader which senses the holes either electrically or optically, translates the reading into electrical impulses, and transmits the impulses into a predefined area in the memory of the computer *on command from the computer. Normally, all 80 columns are read, regardless of whether they contain punches.* Thus, allowance is usually made in the computer memory for storing 80 characters when a card-read command is given.

Output

We shall assume for purposes of this text that the only forms of output being used are either printed line or punched card.

The punched card produced as output is similar in principle to the punched card used for input. A similar rule applies: *All 80 columns may be punched,* so that allowance is usually made in the memory for the storage of 80 adjacent characters (or blanks) to be punched into the blank card supplied by the punch feed mechanism.

The printed line is produced by a variety of electromechanical devices. The common feature is that an entire line is printed in one operation, the maximum length of the line in terms of number of characters depending on the particular model—120 and 132 are common numbers of print positions. Provision must be made in the memory, therefore, for the adjacent storage of the appropriate number of characters in a suitable printout area.

The layout of the fields on the printed line will match exactly the layout of the fields in the predefined printout area in memory.

It should be understood that whereas many of the fields entered into the computer via a punched card may be output on to the printed line, there need be no similarity in the sequence of these fields.

On the other hand, when the output is in the form of punched cards, it is very common for those output fields which are identical to the input fields to be punched in identical columns on the two cards.

Arithmetic and Logic

The means by which the computer hardware performs arithmetic and logic operations is of no direct concern to the programmer. Interested students may refer to the numerous texts available on this topic. The rules for using arithmetic instructions will depend on the particular computer and language being used, and so they are also not dealt with here. However, there are certain general rules and procedures of arithmetic which are covered, more appropriately, in Chapter 5.

Memory and Control

Again, we are not concerned with the technical details of how computer memories work. However, proper understanding of the way in which the memory is to be used is of vital interest to the programmer in his design of the flowchart procedure. The following brief description, studied in conjunction with a manual on coding the computer to which the student has access, should be sufficient for this purpose.

The memory of a computer can store individual characters (numbers, letters, and special symbols) by magnetic means somewhat similar to that of a tape recorder. A given computer memory will have a certain size, i.e., the capability of storing a certain maximum number of characters. Typical numbers would be 4000 on a small computer and as high as 1 million on a large one. As on a tape recorder, *recording* of a new character in a certain position will *erase* the character previously stored there, but *reading* (playback) of a character leaves it *unchanged.*

In a computer memory, unlike a tape-recorder tape, we may wish to record or read out characters in nonsequential order. It is necessary, therefore, to have a means of referring at will to any particular character. This is done by means of its "address," a reference number identifying a particular storage position in the memory. The character stored at a particular storage position may change many times during the execution of a program, but the address of that storage position never changes. Thus, we can picture a computer memory as an array of storage positions referenced by their addresses and containing data which may be constantly changing.

However, in addition to containing data of the type normally handled in a business calculation (e.g., employee number, hours worked, rate of pay, gross pay, etc.), the memory of a computer is also used to store the program. This is the set of instructions, suitably encoded, which the computer must follow in order to read in the input data, perform the calculations, and produce the answers as output. These instructions are stored in the memory in exactly the same way as data are stored. As such, they can be manipulated and changed during the course of the program, resulting in very powerful programming techniques.

The function of Control is to take the set of instructions from the memory, one at a time, in sequence, and execute them, thereby controlling the reading in of data, the performing of calculations, the storing of intermediate results in the memory, and the printing out of final answers in the form of a report.

Naturally, we must take care not to try to store the program and the data in the same storage positions, or the one stored last will erase the other.

In schematic form, then, the memory of a computer performing the simple program of reading an employee's hours and rate from a card, calculating the gross pay, and printing out a line containing the employee number and gross pay could be represented as in Figure 1-3. The corresponding input card and output report formats are illustrated in Figure 1-4.

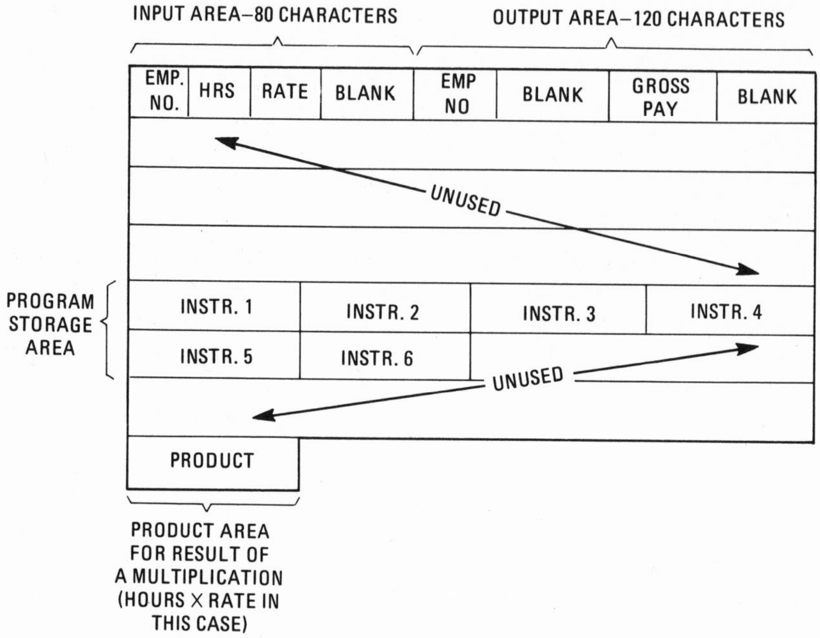

Fig. 1-3. Schematic Representation of Memory for Gross Pay Calculation.

In this example the instructions might be as follows (suitably coded, of course):

INSTR. 1. Read a card into the input area.
INSTR. 2. Multiply hours field by rate field (answer to be placed in a product area).
INSTR. 3. Move answer from product area to appropriate part of output area.
INSTR. 4. Move employee number from input area to output area.
INSTR. 5. Print line from output area.
INSTR. 6. Stop.

These instructions constitute the program, and if followed by the computer (or for that matter by a human operator) they will give the desired result.

Notice the following features.

1. The input area, the output area, and the program storage area can each be

located anywhere in the memory. (Some computers do have certain specific restrictions.)

2. *The instructions must be stored adjacent to each other in correct sequence.* (There are exceptions to this rule as we shall see later when we consider branching.)
3. When the computer is instructed to start processing at INSTRUCTION 1, CONTROL goes to the memory location of INSTRUCTION 1, reads the instruction, and executes it. It then goes *automatically* to INSTRUCTION 2 and repeats the procedure. Then it continues with INSTRUCTION 3 and so on, until it comes to an instruction which says "STOP PROCESSING." Execution of this instruction naturally terminates the procedure. If the programmer forgets to include the STOP instruction, CONTROL will continue to seek the next instruction in the next adjacent memory location and try to execute whatever it finds there. Obviously, in most cases, it will find no meaningful instruction and an error condition will be registered. One situation in which CONTROL will not seek the next instruction in the next adjacent memory location is if it finds a BRANCH instruction such as the UNCONDITIONAL BRANCH. In this case it seeks the next instruction at the memory location specified in the BRANCH instruction. This

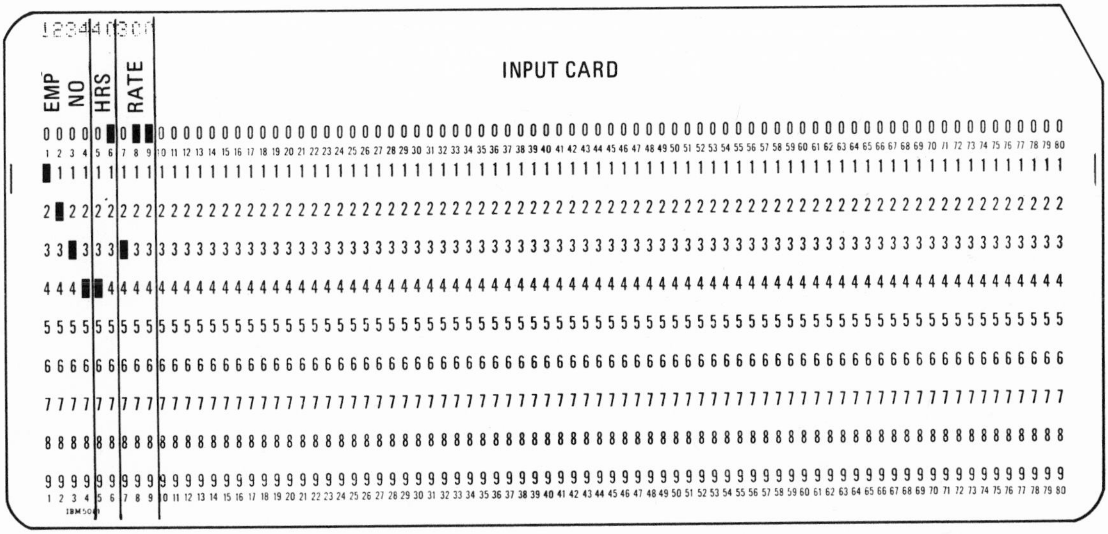

GROSS PAY REPORT

EMP. NO.	GROSS PAY
1234	120.00
1235	110.00
2346	115.00

etc.

Fig. 1-4.

specified location may be anywhere in the memory, thus permitting CONTROL to jump back and forth throughout the memory.

4. In the illustration, it is assumed that the result of the multiplication is stored in a special part of the computer called a product area. This will depend on the particular computer being used. This special area may be a special part of the normal memory, it may be *any* desired part of the normal memory, or it may be a separate piece of hardware.

Basic Flowcharting

With a set of instructions in list form as in the former example, it is not very easy to see quickly and in broad outline the general strategy of a complicated program or to check easily that all steps interconnect logically. This can be done much more readily with the procedure set out in a pictorial form called a flowchart. The advantages of this form may not become apparent until we consider more complex problems, but the student should get into the habit of using it from the beginning. The symbols used are few and are shown in Figure 1-5. The flowchart for our simple problem then becomes as shown in Figure 1-6.

Notice that we have broken down the program into its basic steps. We have represented each of these basic steps by means of the appropriate geometric figure taken from Figure 1-5. We have then entered into each geometric block a brief, plain English description of the function of that step.

In this presentation, we have given first the program and then the flowchart. *From now on, we must realize that this is the reverse of the correct procedure.* The flowchart *must* be produced first and the program coding developed from the flowchart. This is because the flowchart is the best way to analyze the steps required to solve a complicated programming problem.

The subject of flowcharting will be covered in more detail in later chapters. Sufficient information has been given here to enable the student to proceed with elementary problems.

Repetitive Processing

The use of a computer for a simple calculation, such as the preceding example of one employee's gross pay, could hardly be justified. Most business calculations are quite simple, but the justification for use of a computer lies in the fact that the calculations must usually be repeated hundreds or thousands of times. The high speed of operation of a computer then results in an economic process.

If we wished to use our simple program to calculate the gross pay for several thousand employees, we could do so by instructing the computer to go back to the first instruction after printing the data from the first card and repeat the instructions for the second card and again for the third card and so on, *as long as there are more cards to be read in.* The computer can be instructed to do this by means of a "conditional branch" represented by the diamond shape, as shown in Figure 1-7. This contains a question (are there more cards to be read in?) and the subsequent action of the computer depends on the answer to this question.

If there is another card to be processed, the computer is instructed to go back to the first instruction (read a card into the input area)

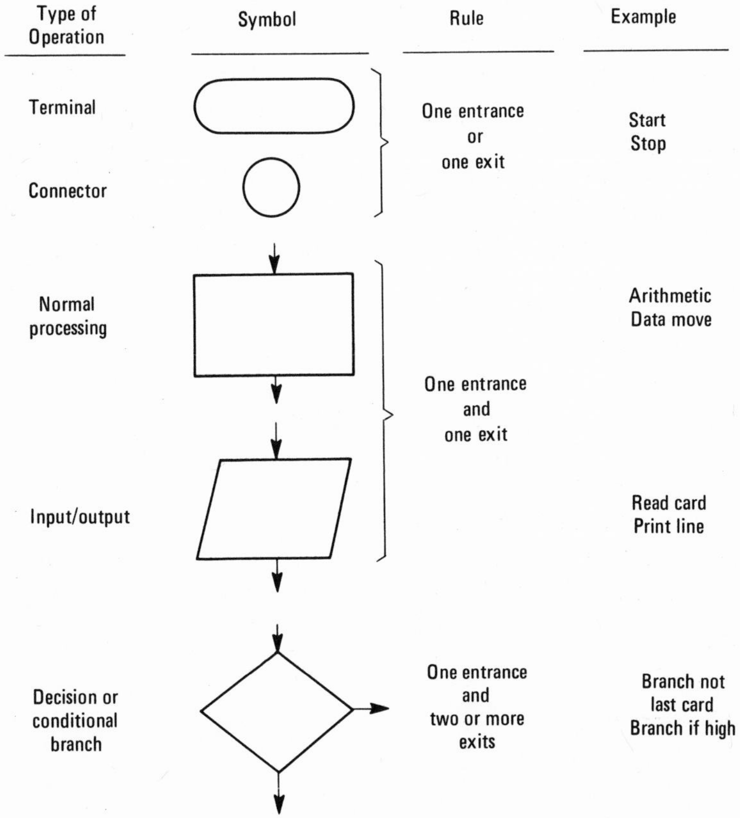
Type of Operation
Symbol
Rule
Example
Terminal
Connector
One entrance or one exit
Start
Stop
Normal processing
Arithmetic
Data move
One entrance and one exit
Input/output
Read card
Print line
Decision or conditional branch
One entrance and two or more exits
Branch not last card
Branch if high

Fig. 1-5. Most Commonly Used Flowcharting Symbols.

followed by the second instruction, and so on. Note that the second card is read into the same input area as was the first card. The data from the first card is, therefore, erased and all its information is lost to the computer memory.

If there are no more cards to be processed, the computer recognizes this condition and does not branch back to the first instruction. Instead it goes to the STOP instruction and the job is terminated.

(The operation of the flowchart can be visualized as like that of a model railway layout with the train beginning at the START operation and continuing along the lines of flow, being diverted one way or another by switches, possibly even looping back to the START operation, but proceeding without pause until it reaches a STOP instruction.)

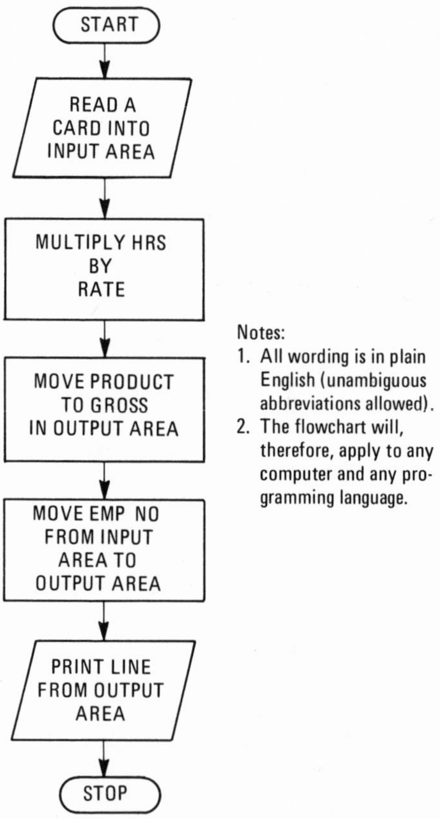
START
READ A CARD INTO INPUT AREA
MULTIPLY HRS BY RATE
MOVE PRODUCT TO GROSS IN OUTPUT AREA
MOVE EMP NO FROM INPUT AREA TO OUTPUT AREA
PRINT LINE FROM OUTPUT AREA
STOP
Notes:
1. All wording is in plain English (unambiguous abbreviations allowed).
2. The flowchart will, therefore, apply to any computer and any programming language.

Fig. 1-6. Flowchart for Calculation of an Employee's Gross Pay.

Let us see now how this flowchart would be converted into a coded program using a self-explanatory coding language called PLC. The coding is divided into two sections. One section deals with the executable instructions, i.e., the actual sequential steps the computer goes through. The other section deals with the definitions (usually called "declaratives") of the data-storage areas in the memory.

Both sections are divided into four columns marked LABEL, OPERATION, OPERANDS, and COMMENTS.

In the instructions section each line represents one executable instruction. The first column may be used, if required, to give the

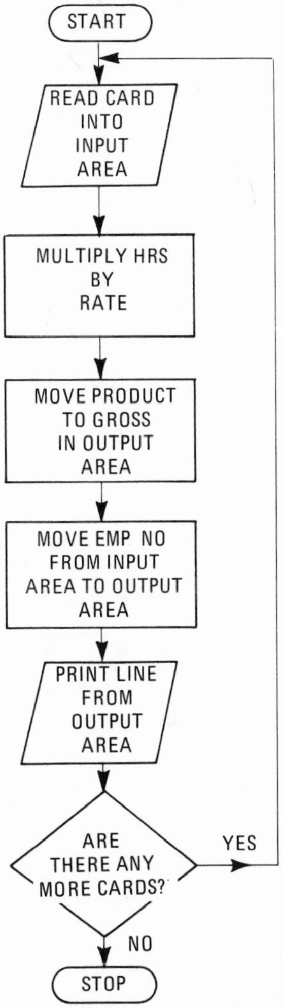

Fig. 1-7. Flowchart for Calculation of Several Employees' Gross Pay.

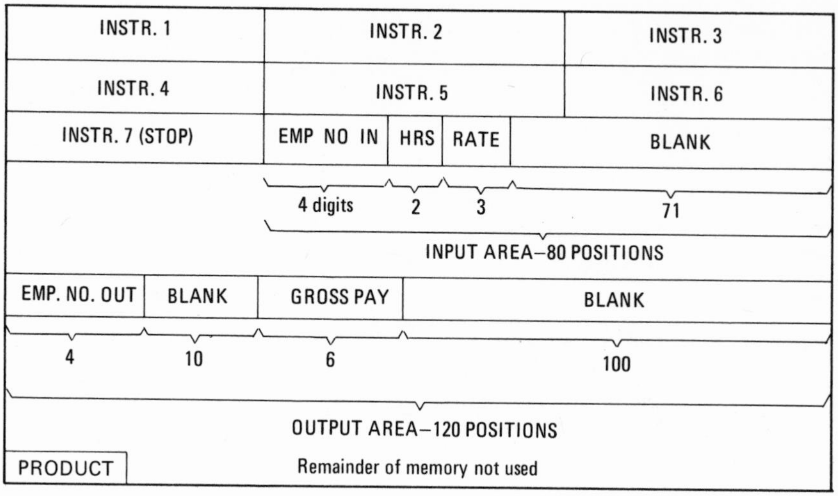

Fig. 1-8. Arrangement of Memory for Illustrative PLC Coding of Fig. 1-7.

instruction a label or name, so that the instruction can be referred to by that label elsewhere in the program. Thus, in the PLC coding that follows, the sixth instruction refers back to the first instruction by using its label "START."

The second column specifies the type of operation that the instruction is to execute, e.g., READ CARD, MULT (meaning multiply), MOVE, ADD, etc.

The operands column specifies the data fields on which the operation is to be performed or, in the case of a branch type instruction, the name of the instruction which is to be executed if the branch is to be taken.

The comments column is for recording any useful information the programmer wishes and has no effect on the execution.

In the declaratives section, each line is used to define an area in the memory for the storage of data. A large area, such as an 80-position input area, may be subdivided into smaller areas for individual fields.

The first column is again used to give the area defined a reference label. This will be used in the operands column of the executable instructions to specify the required data.

The second column indicates by the word DEFINE that this is a declarative and not an executable instruction.

The operands column specifies the size of the data area and its location within a larger area, if it is a subdivision.

PLC Coding of Figure 1-7

LABEL	*OPERATION*	*OPERANDS*	*COMMENTS*
		Instructions	
START	READ CARD	INTO INPUT	We need a label for this instruction since we shall be branching back to it
	MULT	HOURS BY RATE	Hours and rate are stored in INPUT; answer is gross pay in product area
	MOVE	PRODUCT TO GROSSPAY	The answer is moved to the output area
	MOVE	EMP. NO. IN TO EMP. NO.	The employee number is moved to the output area
	PRINT LINE	FROM OUTPUT	One line of the report is printed
	BNLC	TO START	This instruction checks to see if there are more data cards to be processed; if so, the computer goes back to the first instruction; otherwise, it goes to the next instruction
	STOP		End of job
		Definitions	
INPUT	DEFINE	80	The input area is defined as 80 storage positions long
EMP. NO. IN	DEFINE	INPUT (1-4)	The first four positions of the input area will contain the emp. no.
HOURS	DEFINE	INPUT (5-6)	Positions 5 and 6 of the input area contain the hours
RATE	DEFINE	INPUT (7-9)	Positions 7-9 of input area contain the rate
	DEFINE	INPUT (10-80)	The remaining 71 positions need not be named
OUTPUT	DEFINE	120	The output area is defined as 120 storage positions long
EMP. NO. OUT	DEFINE	OUTPUT (1-4)	The first four positions of the output area will contain the emp. no.
	DEFINE	OUTPUT (5-14)	These positions are not named and will be left blank
GROSSPAY	DEFINE	OUTPUT (15-20)	Six positions are allocated for printing the gross pay
	DEFINE	OUTPUT (21-120)	The remaining positions will be left blank

The comments column fulfills the same function as in the executable instructions section.

Figure 1-8 shows schematically the layout of the memory for this program. Note that the layout is different from that of Figure 1-3. This is purely to illustrate the flexibility with which the memory can be used.

Totals

Usually in repetitive processing of a deck of cards we wish to accumulate totals. These may be an essential part of the output information or they may be required for purposes of control, i.e., to ensure that all the correct cards, and only the correct cards, have been processed. This may be readily accomplished by setting aside a part of the memory, or a suitable register, for accumulation of the total and writing it out at the end of the job. It is considered good practice to make certain that this accumulator is cleared to zero at the start of the job (i.e., *before* the READ A CARD instruction). (Why not after?) This is called "initializing." Figure 1-9 shows an example of this. The PLC coding follows.

Note the use of the connector Ⓐ at the bottom of the page to show that the flow continues at the other connector Ⓐ at the top right.

Desk Checking

After the programmer has drawn the flowchart and coded the program, the next step is to keypunch the program on cards, usually one card per instruction. The program cards should then be printed on a printer and the listing carefully checked. Many keypunching and coding errors can occur in a program and a great deal of expensive computer time can be saved by a critical check of the program deck, since the slightest error in keypunching or coding will result in an inoperable program. More specific guidance will be given in Chapter 6.

Translating the Source Program

The program as written, and as illustrated in the examples of PLC coding, is known as the "source program." It cannot be executed by the computer as it stands but must be translated into machine language code appropriate to the particular computer. This translation is performed by the computer using a special program supplied by the manufacturer.

The result of this procedure, which is known as assembling or compiling, is an "object program" which can then be executed by the computer.

Appendix C gives a fuller explanation of this process.

Testing and Debugging

Probably one of the most important aspects of program writing is proper testing of the finished program. We can never assume that a program will work, no matter how carefully it is checked. The only safe test is to run it with the computer, feeding in sample test data cards and verifying that the answers produced are exactly as required. If they are not, corrections must be made and the process repeated until completely satisfactory results are obtained.

The amount of time that will be spent on testing may vary from 10% of the total to 80%, depending on the ability of the programmer. Experience shows, however, that the more time spent on initial program analysis, the less time required for testing and debugging.

Documentation

Finally, the program will be made to work satisfactorily and can be handed over to the operating staff. In addition, however, a complete record of all the information acquired and used in preparation of the program must be assembled and filed for future reference. This recording or "documentation" is described in detail in Chapter 8.

PROGRAM WRITING

We can now summarize the main steps in writing a computer program (including getting it to work).

1. Define the Problem. This is often the task requiring the most

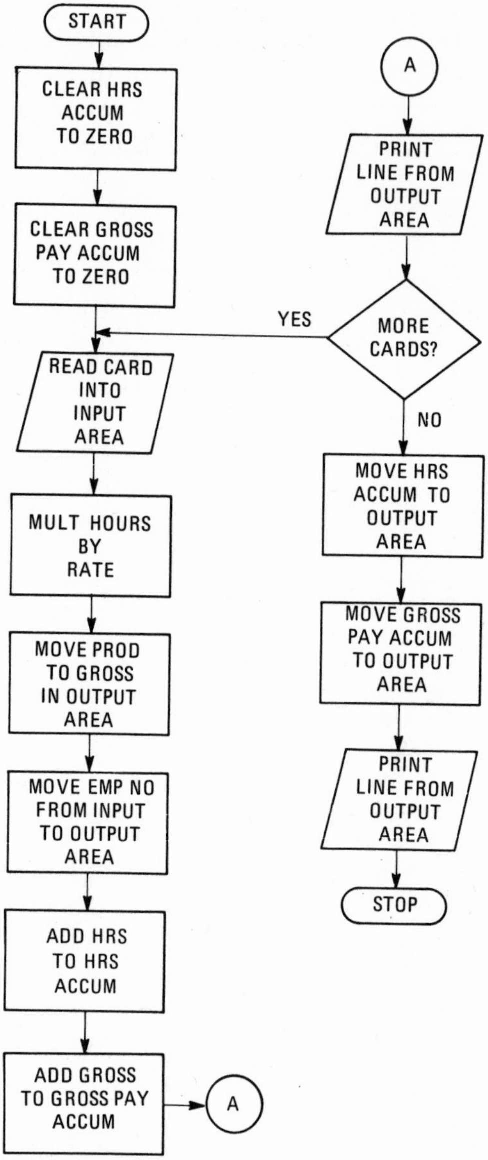

Fig. 1-9. Flowchart for Calculation of Many Employees' Gross Pay with Accumulated Totals.

PLC Coding of Figure 1-9

LABEL	*OPERATION*	*OPERANDS*	*COMMENTS*
		Instructions	
START	CLEAR	HOURSACCUM	Initializing
	CLEAR	GROSSACCUM	
BEGIN	READ CARD	INTO INPUT	
	MULT	HOURS BY RATE	
	MOVE	PRODUCT TO GROSSPAY	
	MOVE	EMP. NO. IN TO EMP. NO. OUT	Note the difference between a MOVE instruction and an ADD instruction
	ADD	HOURS TO HOURSACCUM	
	ADD	GROSS TO GROSSACCUM	
	PRINT LINE	FROM OUTPUT	
	BNLC	BEGIN	Note that in this example we branch to BEGIN, not START
	MOVE	HOURSACCUM TO OUTPUT (2-5)	Total hours is to be printed in positions 2-5
	MOVE	GROSSACCUM TO OUTPUT (13-20)	Total pay is to be printed in positions 13-20
	PRINT LINE	FROM OUTPUT	
	STOP		
		Definitions	
INPUT	DEFINE	80	
EMP. NO. IN	DEFINE	INPUT (1-4)	
HOURS	DEFINE	INPUT (5-6)	
RATE	DEFINE	INPUT (7-9)	
	DEFINE	INPUT (10-80)	
OUTPUT	DEFINE	120	
EMP. NO. OUT	DEFINE	OUTPUT (1-4)	
	DEFINE	OUTPUT (5-14)	
GROSSPAY	DEFINE	OUTPUT (15-20)	
	DEFINE	OUTPUT (21-120)	
HOURSACCUM	DEFINE	4	These declaratives define two areas in which total hours & total pay are to be accumulated
GROSSACCUM	DEFINE	8	

attention and given the least. It should be apparent that if all details of a problem are not clearly understood, there can be little hope of developing a satisfactory program.

In particular, a clear understanding of the nature and form of the information being fed into the system and of the output required from the system is essential.

2. Formulate a Solution–Flowchart. The preparation of a solution in the form of a flowchart has several advantages:

a. It promotes clear, logical analysis of the solution by its easy-to-follow representation.
b. It makes communication of the solution to others easy.
c. It provides a good form of permanent documentation of the solution.

3. Code. The important point here is that the program coding *must follow* the procedure outlined on the flowchart. If the flowchart is correct, and if the coding follows the flowchart, and if there are no errors in coding, then the program will work. (Unfortunately it seems to be very rare for these three conditions to be met.)

4. Desk Check. After a program has been coded and keypunched, the cards should be checked for obvious errors. The desirable extent of this checking is a matter of opinion. The availability of computer time and other factors should be taken into account.

5. Test and Debug. One of the rules of programming is that "no program can be expected to work the first time." It is essential, therefore, that all programs be thoroughly tested with test data simulating all possible conditions. Naturally, any errors discovered must be corrected, and after *every* such correction *all tests must be repeated.* It is deceptively easy to correct one error and in so doing to introduce another.

6. Document the Job. More on this is provided in Chapter 8 and is illustrated in Appendix B.

PROBLEMS

PROBLEM 1-1 (mandatory)

Employees' Net Pay Report

Write the program, get it to work on your computer, and prepare complete documentation for the problem given below. This includes:

1. Diagram of memory allocation (as in Fig. 1-3)
2. Flowchart
3. Compiled program listing
4. Listing of test data cards
5. Listing of answers for test data
6. Proof of correctness of answers

INPUT

A deck of cards containing

	CARD COLUMNS
Employee number	1-5
Employee's gross pay	6-11
Income tax deduction	12-17
Union dues	18-22
Other deductions	23-27

OUTPUT

1. One printed line (or punched card) for each employee containing all input information and net pay (columns 75-80 if on cards)
2. One printed line (or punched card) showing *total* net pay for all employees (card columns 73-80)

HINT

Since all input information must be retained for output, arithmetic must be done in some other area. Treat this area as though it were an adding machine. Make sure it is zero to start with and then add or subtract each item into it, one at a time.

PROBLEM 1-2

Discount on Accounts Payable

Write a program to calculate the discount and net amount owing on accounts payable cards.

INPUT

A deck of cards, each containing

	CARD COLUMNS
Vendor number	1-5
Amount owing (XXXXXX.XX)	11-18
Discount rate (XX.X% = .XXX)	21-23

OUTPUT

One printed line for each card showing vendor number, amount, discount rate, discount, and net, with totals for all money amount columns.

HINT

The result of multiplying dollars and cents by the discount rate will have decimal places denoting tenths, hundredths, and thousandths of a cent (see Chapter 5). Simply ignore these unwanted decimals in the answer.

2

Conditional Branching

It is quite often stated that the computer has the power of making choices or decisions. This is not as mysterious as it may sound since it merely refers to the execution of the type of instruction called a conditional branch. We have already seen one example of this in the previous chapter under the heading Repetitive Processing and in Figure 1-7. Here the computer was instructed to branch back to the start of the program if there were more cards to be processed. Otherwise it was to stop.

COMPARE AND BRANCH

Another very common use of the conditional branch is in the choice between two alternative courses of action depending on the result of the comparison of the value of two numbers. Suppose, for instance, that a sales manager wished to know which of his customers purchased a volume of more than $1000 worth of goods in a certain period. The computer could be instructed to read a card containing a customer's number and volume of sales. The latter could be compared to the number 1000.00. If it recognized that the amount of sales were higher, the computer would branch to an instruction which would print out, or punch out on a card, the details of that particular customer and then return to the beginning of the program to process the next card (if any). If the amount were not higher, that customer would be ignored and the next card (if any) processed. The flowchart would be as in Figure 2-1.

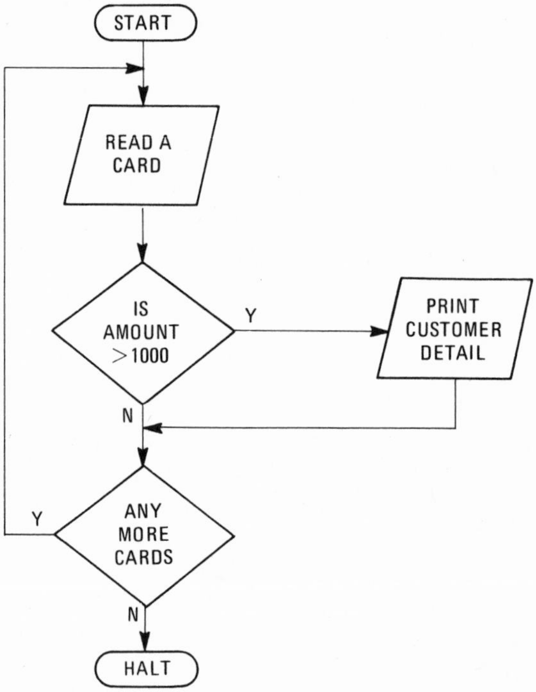

Fig. 2-1. Simple Compare and Branch Program.

Notice that in this type of comparison there are three possible results:

1. Sales volume *greater than* 1000.00 (sales $>$ 1000.00–note that the wide end of the symbol $>$ is next to the larger number).
2. Sales volume *less than* 1000.00 (sales $<$ 1000.00).
3. Sales volume *equal to* 1000.00 (sales = 1000.00).

CODING THE CONDITIONAL BRANCH

In the flowchart, the conditional branch is shown by the single geometric figure the diamond. Except in special cases, however (such as the last card branch instructions–BLC, BNLC), it will require at least two machine instructions to be coded in assembler-type languages.

The first instruction will be a COMPARE instruction specifying the fields to be compared as operands. In most computers execution of this command results in the setting of indicators or condition codes, depending on the results of the comparison. The second and possibly third instructions will tell the computer to branch or not, depending on the state of the indicators. Thus the relevant part of our example in Figure 2-1 would be coded in PLC as follows:

LABEL	*OPERATION*	*OPERANDS*	*COMMENTS*
START	. . .		
	COMPARE	SALES TO 1000.00	
	BRANCH IF NOT HIGH	TO LAST	
	PRINT LINE	FROM OUTPUT	
LAST	BNLC	START	
	. . .		

Notice that in PLC coding, the condition specified in the BRANCH instruction refers to the first operand in the COMPARE instruction, i.e., in the above example the BRANCH instruction is taken to mean

BRANCH TO LAST IF SALES is NOT HIGHer than 1000.00

Some coding languages work in the reverse manner. Thus care is necessary to avoid errors.

It is important to ensure that the flowchart and program operate correctly in all possible situations. This is facilitated in most computers by the availability of seven different branch instructions, one or more of which will prove appropriate in every case. These are usually as follows:

Branch low	BL
Branch not low	BNL
Branch equal	BE
Branch not equal	BNE
Branch high	BH
Branch not high	BNH
Branch unconditionally	B

Notice the following points:

1. "High or equal" is logically the same as "not low" and "low or equal" is the same as "not high." Thus the following two examples of coding will give identical results.

LABEL	*OPERATION*	*OPERANDS*	*COMMENTS*
	COMPARE	A TO B	
	BH	LATER	Branch to LATER if high or equal
	BE	LATER	
	. . .		Carry on without branching if low
LATER			

LABEL	*OPERATION*	*OPERANDS*	*COMMENTS*
	COMPARE	A TO B	
	BNL	LATER	Branch to LATER if not low
	. . .		Carry on if low
LATER			

2. A comparison of A with B followed by "branch high" is the same logically as a comparison of B with A followed by a "branch low." Thus the following two examples of coding will give identical results.

LABEL	*OPERATION*	*OPERANDS*	*COMMENTS*
	COMPARE	A TO B	
	BH	LATER	
	. . .		
LATER			

LABEL	*OPERATION*	*OPERANDS*	*COMMENTS*
	COMPARE	B TO A	
	BL	LATER	
	. . .		
LATER			

Caution should be exercised in dealing with the type of problem which requires more than one comparison before a decision can be made. For instance, is the sales volume greater than $1000.00 but less than $10,000.00? A flowchart should be drawn and carefully checked to ensure that the correct action is taken in all cases.

Example 2-1

An insurance company wishes to extract certain information from its files. Each card record includes the following information:

	COLUMNS
Policy number	1-8
Age	9-10
Sex code (1 male, 2 female)	11
Occupation code	12-13

Required is printed line (output card) for each record of a male, either over the age of 50 with an occupation code between the numbers 23 and 27 inclusive or with age equal to 50.

The output is to contain only the policy number.

Solution: The flowchart is as shown in Figure 2-2.

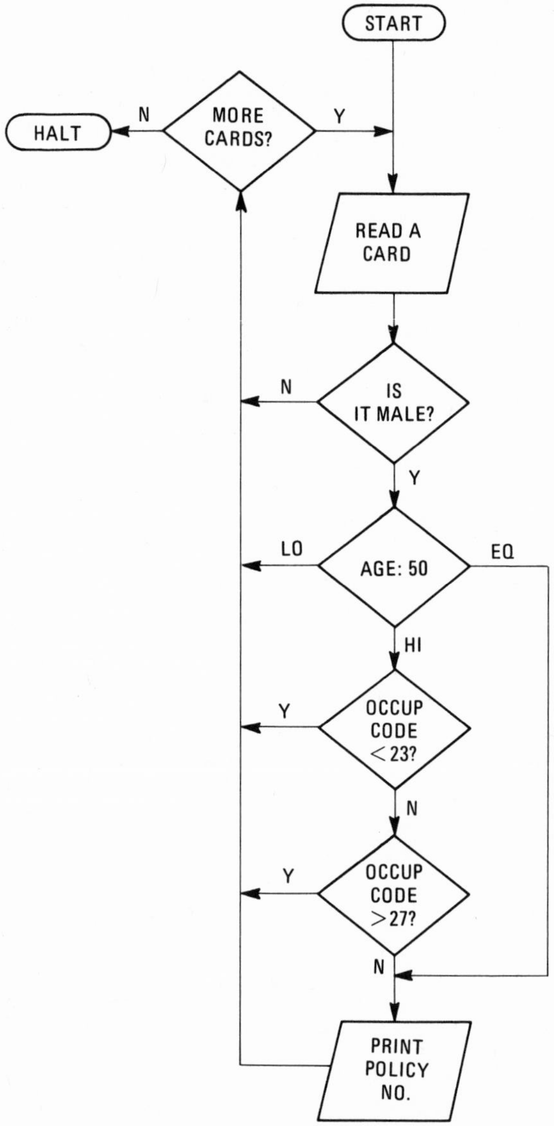

NOTE: AGE: 50 is an abbreviation for COMPARE AGE TO 50

Fig. 2-2. Example 2-1, Conditional Branching.

PLC Coding of Example 2-1

LABEL	*OPERATION*	*OPERANDS*	*COMMENTS*
START	READ CARD	INTO INPUT	
	COMPARE	SEX TO '1'	Testing for "male"
	BNE	LAST	If not male, no further action on this card
	COMPARE	AGE TO '50'	
	BE	PRINTOUT	If male and age 50, printout required
	BL	LAST	If under 50, no further action on this card
	COMPARE	OCCUP TO '23'	
	BL	LAST	If occupation $<$ 23, no further action
	COMPARE	OCCUP TO '27'	
	BH	LAST	If occupation $>$ 27, no further action
PRINTOUT	MOVE	POLICYNO TO OUTPUT	
	PRINT LINE	FROM OUTPUT	
LAST	BNLC	START	
	HALT		

Reviewing this coded example, we see that after the first instruction has read in a data card, the sex code is compared to 1 to check for a record of a male. If it is not 1, we are not interested in the record further and so wish to go to the last card test preparatory to reading the next card.

We see from the flowchart that we shall be branching to this last card test from several other points in the program, so it seems reasonable to put this test at the end of the coding, give it the label LAST, and branch not equal in this case.

If the code is equal to 1, the computer will not branch to LAST but will go to the next instruction. This must be the age comparison, which is coded next.

Following COMPARE, we have three possibilities. If the age is equal to 50, we require a printout, so we code a branch to the instruction PRINTOUT, which we see from the flowchart will occur after the checks on occupation code. If the age is less than 50, we are not interested further in this record, and so the branch equal instruction must be followed by a branch low to LAST. If the age is greater than 50, neither branch will be taken and the computer will proceed to the next instruction.

We see from the flowchart that this will be a comparison of the occupation code to 23. Coding of this section of the flowchart follows a similar pattern, as does the subsequent comparison to 27. A low comparison here brings us to the printout instruction followed by the last card test and the final HALT.

Testing

A suitable set of test data cards would be as follows:

POLICY NUMBER	*AGE*	*SEX CODE*	*OCCUPATION CODE*
12345678	50	2	26
23456789	27	1	19
34567890	50	1	26
45678901	51	1	19
56789012	51	1	23
67890123	51	1	25
78901234	51	1	30
89012345	51	1	27
90123456	51	2	19

Notice that every possible path in the flowchart is tested by at least one card.

RECOMMENDED PRACTICES

1. In the flowcharting, the wording in the decision diamond should make plain English sense so that there is no ambiguity. This can be done in two ways (see Figure 2-2):

a. The diamond contains a question (e.g., is occupation code less than the value 23), and the two exits are each marked with the appropriate answer, which will be YES or NO.

b. The diamond contains the expression AGE: 50 (age compared to 50) or the instruction COMPARE AGE TO 50, and the exits are marked with the appropriate results of the comparison, i.e., HI, LO, =. Do not put something like BNH in the diamond with YES or NO on the two exits. This is ambiguous.

2. Where there are a number of conditional branches in a program, decide on a logical procedure for laying out the flowchart so as to produce a clear, easy to follow result. A good plan, where appropriate, is to make the straight-line main flow of the diagram deal with the most likely situation and complete this part of the flowchart first.

3. In coding, use the procedure which will result in the most straightforward and easy to follow program, with the minimum of jumping around. This can be done by making an intelligent choice between the two options of branching on the condition being tested or branching on the opposite condition (e.g., BH or BNH). Both choices can be made to work and give the right answers, but one will give a neater and clearer program than the other.

For example, the first few instructions of Example 2-1 could have been coded as follows:

LABEL	*OPERATION*	*OPERANDS*	*COMMENTS*
START	READ CARD	INTO INPUT	
	COMPARE	SEX TO '1'	
	BE	STEP2	
	B	LAST	
STEP2	COMPARE	AGE TO '50'	
	etc.		

Obviously, the method shown previously is simpler and more efficient. Problem 2-1 (at the end of this chapter) may now be attempted.

ERROR ROUTINES

The ability of the computer to compare numbers and then to branch depending on the result gives it a great capability for detecting errors that may arise in a real-life data-processing situation. For instance, punched cards representing employees' time tickets may be required to have a "card code" punched in a certain column (often column 1 or 80) to identify them. Occasionally, due to human error, a card without the appropriate punch may get into the deck. Therefore, whenever these cards are processed through the computer, the card code on each card should be checked to ensure that such an error is detected. This would be done by comparing the code with the known correct value and branching if not equal to a set of instructions known as an "error routine." These instructions would take the most appropriate action, such as writing out an error message and then continuing with the next data card, or terminating the job, etc.

Such techniques should be used whenever possible, since the cost in operating time is extremely small and the saving when an error is detected can be considerable. Other examples are correct date, limiting values (on checks, customers' balances, etc.), valid customer account numbers, and sequence errors. (See Chapter 10.) Problems 2-2 and 2-3 may now be attempted.

SEQUENCE CHECKING

Most of the files used in a data-processing system will be in some kind of numeric sequence such as employee number, customer number, stock number, ledger number, etc., with the lowest numbers first followed by the higher numbers. For many operations it is essential that this sequence be correct. It is, therefore, convenient to use the computer's checking ability to verify the sequence whenever the cards are processed.

This can be done by comparing the control or identifying number on the card just read in with the number on the previous card and then branching to an error routine if the former is lower than the latter (for increasing-sequence files). However, the reading in of the new card destroys the value of the prior card stored in the input area. Therefore, before the new card is read in, the number of the old card must be transferred to some storage area outside of the input area so that it will still be available for the comparison. Then, after the comparison, the new number will be transferred to the storage area ready for the reading in of the next card, and so on. The flowchart is shown in Figure 2-3. This flowchart also shows the cards being checked for a valid card code of 1 in card column 1. Invalid cards are being bypassed and an error message is typed out.

After a sequence error has been detected, it is usually necessary to cancel the job, re-sort the input data, and restart the job. With manually operated (i.e., non "operating system") computers this will be facilitated if the error halt is followed by a branch back to start, as indicated by the dotted line and the connector A10.

LAST CARD TEST

The flowcharts presented so far have assumed that the computer, such as the IBM 1620 and 1401, has a last card indicator of some type which is turned on when the last data card is read in and which can be tested by a conditional branch instruction. Many computers, such as the IBM 360, do not have this feature. The fact that all the data cards have been read must then be ascertained by the use of a *trailer card* (which may, in fact, be one of the job control cards in an "operating system" environment).

The trailer card is a dummy data card containing some identifying number known to be *not* present in any *valid* data card (e.g., a negative or zero account number or a "nines" account number such as 9999). As each card is read, a test of this number is made using a compare instruction with a branch on equal to the end of job routine. Figure 2-4 illustrates this. Notice that the last card test now

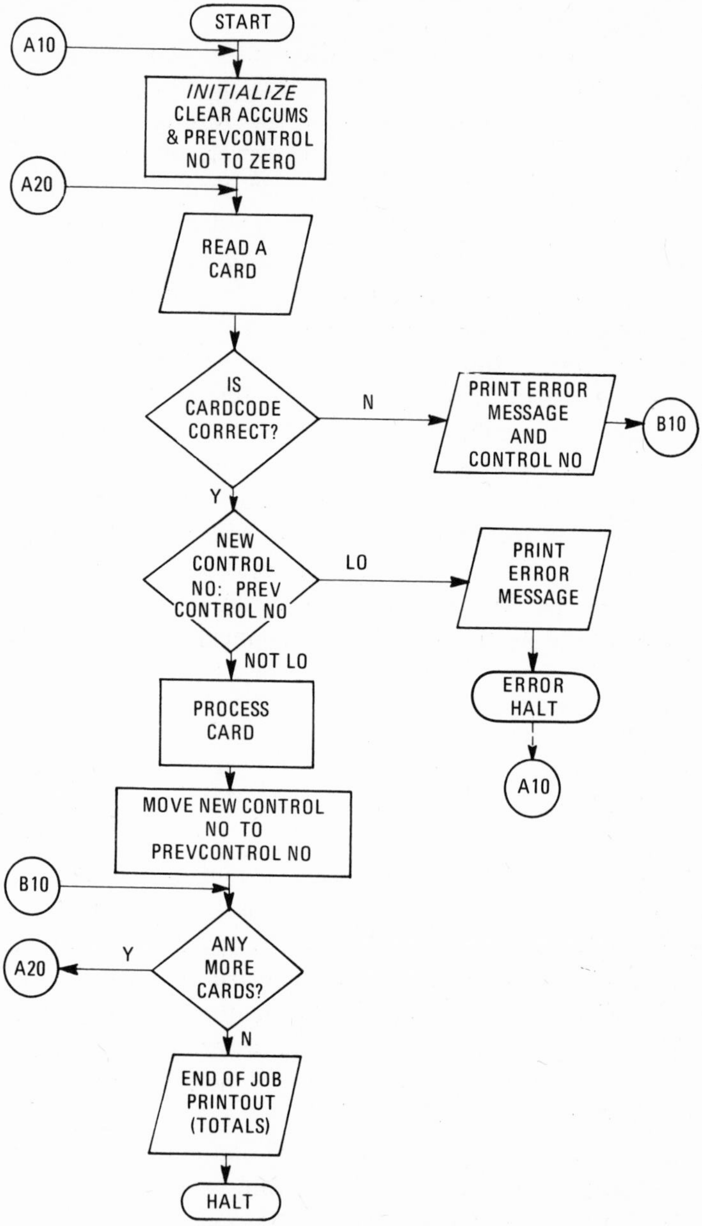

Fig. 2-3. Sequence Checking (Including Card Code Check).

PLC Coding of Figure 2-3 Sequence Checking

LABEL	*OPERATION*	*OPERAND*	*COMMENTS*
A10	CLEAR . . .	ACCUM	One such instruction for each accumulator
	CLEAR	PREVIOUSCONTROL	
A20	READ CARD	INTO INPUT	
	COMPARE	CARDCODE TO '1'	
	BNE	TO E10	
	COMPARE	NEWCONTROL TO PREVIOUSCONTROL	
	BL	TO E20	
	. . .		Arithmetic and other processing of valid card
	MOVE	NEWCONTROL TO PREVIOUSCONTROL	
B10	BNLC	TO A20	
	. . .		End of job printout routine
	STOP		
E10	MOVE	'INVALID CARD CODE' TO OUTPUT }	Invalid card
	MOVE	NEWCONTROL TO OUTPUT }	routine
	PRINT LINE	FROM OUTPUT }	
	B	TO B10	Branch to B10 for next instruction
E20	MOVE	'SEQUENCE ERROR' TO OUTPUT }	Sequence error
	PRINT LINE	FROM OUTPUT }	routine
	STOP		
	B	TO A10	Branch to A10; go back to A10 for next instruction

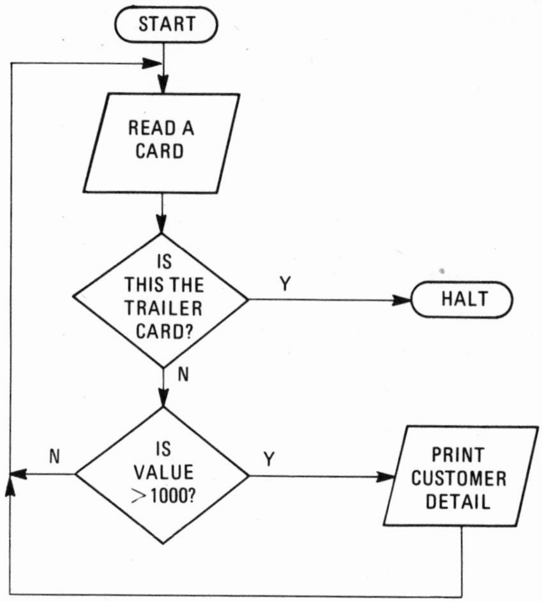

Fig. 2-4. Revision of Figure 2-1 for Use of Trailer Card as Last Card Test.

comes immediately *after* the READ CARD instruction instead of at the end of the processing.

Notice now in Figure 2-3 that after the printout of the invalid card code message, the program cannot branch back to the READ CARD instruction at A20 but must go to the last card test at B10. There is a tendency to overlook this point in a complex flowchart, resulting in error. To overcome this, it is suggested that in this case the last card test should be made immediately *prior* to the READ CARD instruction. This is not as illogical as it may at first seem, since by so doing we ensure that we never issue a READ instruction without having first made sure that there is, in fact, a card to be read. The simple compare and branch program now appears as in Figure 2-5 for the case of a computer with a last card indicator.

The two flowcharts in Figures 2-4 and 2-5 are now identical except that in the former (trailer card method) the last card test is immediately *after* the READ, whereas in the latter (last card indicator method) it is immediately *before* the READ.

For the remainder of this text we shall continue with the assumption that we have a last card indicator. If your computer does not have one, remember to make the appropriate change in the location of the last card test.

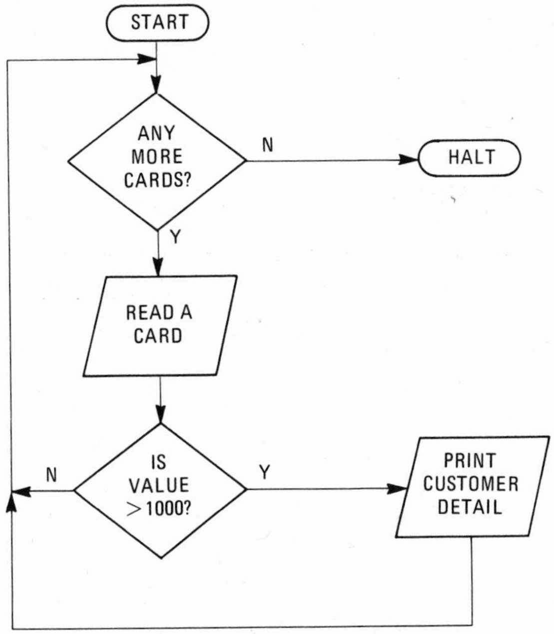

Fig. 2-5. Revision of Figure 2-1 for Recommended Use of Last Card Indicator.

PROBLEMS

PROBLEM 2-1 (mandatory)

Flowchart and code in PLC the following independent segments of a program (assume that the numbers are already stored in the memory in suitable form):

1. Compare X and Y. If X > Y, then go to J10OUT.
2. If both X and Y are less than Z, go to C30.
3. If the larger of X and Y is greater than Z and X is smaller than W, then go to A10.

PROBLEM 2-2 (mandatory)

Income Tax

Flowchart and code a program to calculate Federal Income Tax for taxable incomes less than $10,000. Include an error routine for input data of more than $10,000. Assume that tax is calculated according to the following table:

TAXABLE INCOME ($)	*TAX ($)*
0-2000	10% of taxable income
2001-4000	$200 + 15% of amount over 2000
4001-6000	$500 + 20% of amount over 4000
6001-8000	$900 + 22% of amount over 6000
8001-10000	$1340 + 25% of amount over 8000

Output: Should include employee number, taxable income, and tax payable. Design your own report.

Input: On punched cards each containing employee number in columns 1-4 and taxable income in dollars only in columns 5-9. Sequence check by employee.

At least six test cards will be necessary, one to test for each possible branch.

Full documentation (as in Problem 1-1) should be prepared.

Get this program to work on your computer.

PROBLEM 2-3 (flowchart mandatory)

Write a program to calculate the net pay for each employee, the total cash needed to pay the employees, and the total tax to be remitted to the tax department.

INPUT

One card per employee containing

	CARD COLUMNS
Employee number	1-4
Hours worked (XX.X)	5-7
Rate per hour (X.XX)	8-10
Card code ("4")	80

Time worked over 40 hours is paid at time and one half. Tax is calculated at a flat rate of 20%.

OUTPUT

Design your own report.
Check for valid card code.

PROBLEM 2-4

Draw the flowchart for the following problem: A percentage of sales is offered to salesmen as commission. The percentage differs depending on whether the item sold is class A, B, or C.

Compute the commission amount on the following basis:

1. If the item sold is class A and the volume sold is less than or equal to 1000, the commission is 5% of sales. If greater than 1000, but less than or equal to 3000, the commission is 7% of the sales amount. If greater than 3000, the commission is 10% of the sales amount.
2. If the item sold is class B and the volume sold is less than 1000, the commission is 4% of the sales amount; otherwise, it is 6%.
3. If the item sold is class C, the commission is $4\frac{1}{2}$% of the sales amount.
4. If the item sold is not class A, B, or C, stop.

INPUT

Each input card contains one sale, stating salesman number, class, and volume sold. Salesman numbers are in numeric sequence.

OUTPUT

One line is to be printed for every input card, containing all input data as well as the calculated commission amount. The sequence of cards is to be checked.

3

Control Break: Processing Groups of Cards

Up to now we have considered repetitive processing of individual cards, each one being processed identically to all the others and yet independently of all the others. The one exception was the case of sequence checking, where we compared each card with the one that went before to make sure that this sequence was correct. In practice, a much more usual situation that arises in the vast majority of business problems is one in which the cards are broken down into groups and the cards in a group are to be processed as a group.

For example, we might have all the daily time cards for a week's work grouped together by employee number and be required to calculate each employee's total gross pay for the week by accumulating figures from all his cards. This would then be repeated for the next employee and so on. See Figure 3-1, which shows three cards for employee number 1234, two for employee number 1235, etc. The result would be what is called a tabulation by employee number, or minor totals by employee number.

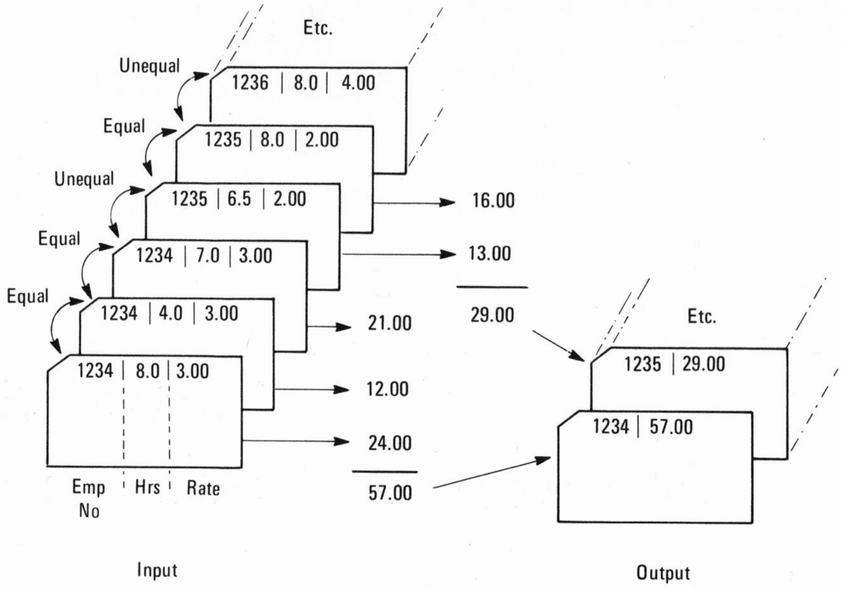

Fig. 3-1. Control Break—Tabulation by Employee Number.

CONTROL BREAK COMPARISON

Notice that the employee numbers are in numeric sequence. The reason is that the simplest way of grouping similar numbers together is by sorting the entire deck on a card-sorting machine. This is usually, also, the most convenient way of filing the cards, since any particular employee's cards can then be readily located. The procedure then is to process each card of a group, constantly checking to see if it is the last card of that group. This condition is indicated when the first card of the next group is read into the input area and its control number is found to be higher than that of the previous card. This indicates a *control break*. (See Figure 3-2.) At this point individual card processing is halted and the terminal group processing (e.g., printout of the group total and its control number and clearing of the group accumulator) is carried out. The control number of the card in the input area is then transferred to the storage area for the "previous control number" and the processing of the input record is resumed. A common programming error at this point is to branch to read the next card and thereby to omit processing the card that initiated the control break.

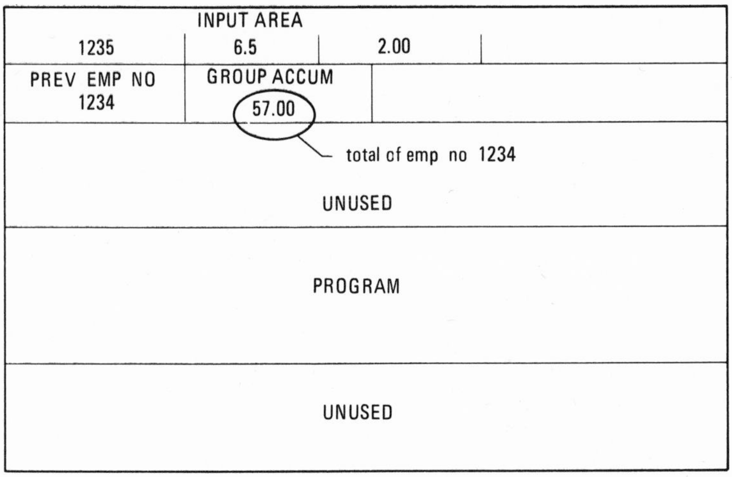

Fig. 3-2. Contents of Memory Immediately after First Card of Employee Number 1235 Has Been Read.

The flowchart (Figure 3-3) shows the basic procedure. Notice two unsatisfactory features of this flowchart:

1. The reading of the first card initiates a control break since the previous control number at this point is zero. This results in an unwanted output of a zero amount for a zero control number.
2. The entire output routine has to be repeated for the last group when the last card is detected. This output routine might in practice amount to a page or two of instructions.

These two problems are characteristic of most multicard programs. Special attention must always be paid to the very first and very last cards processed to ensure that their processing is correct.

There are several ways in which the disadvantages mentioned can be overcome.

SWITCHES

One method is by the use of "switches." A "switch" in this context is a storage position or area which can contain one of two alternative items of information, one item defining the switch as "on" and the

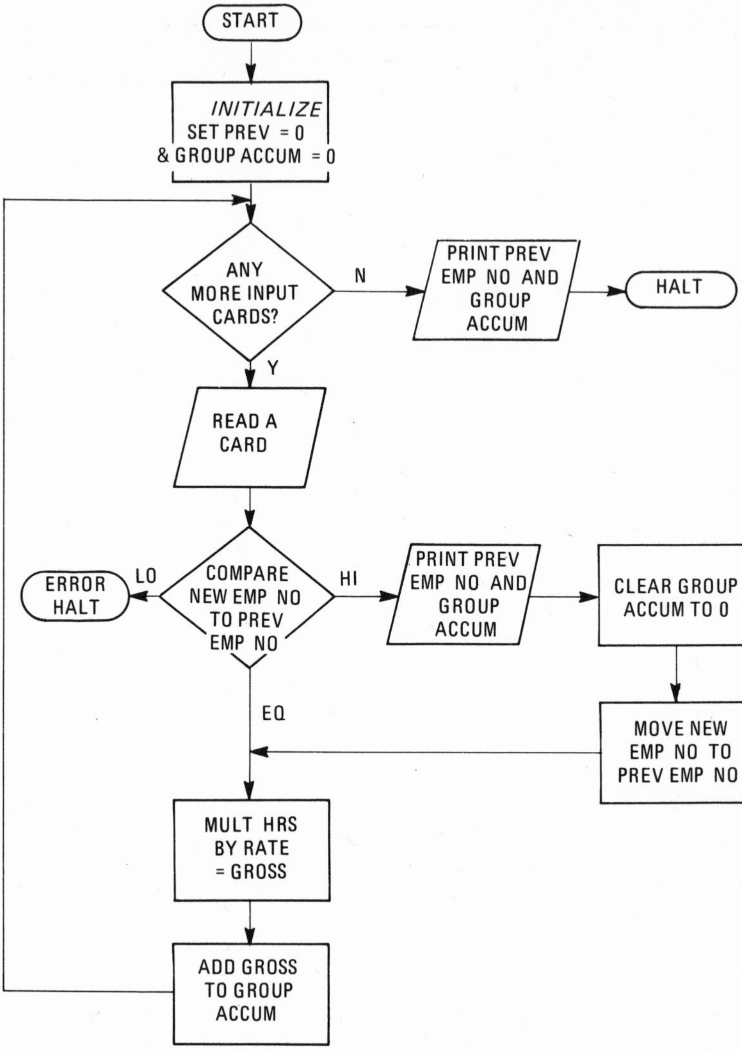

Fig. 3-3. Simple Control Break with Unsatisfactory Processing of the First and Last Cards.

other defining it as "off." For example, a single storage position containing a digit (1-9) indicates the on condition and a zero indicates the off condition.

Figure 3-4 shows the revised flowchart using a first card switch to bypass the unwanted print out of the zero total of the previous group on the first card and a last card switch to avoid the duplication of the output routine on the last card.

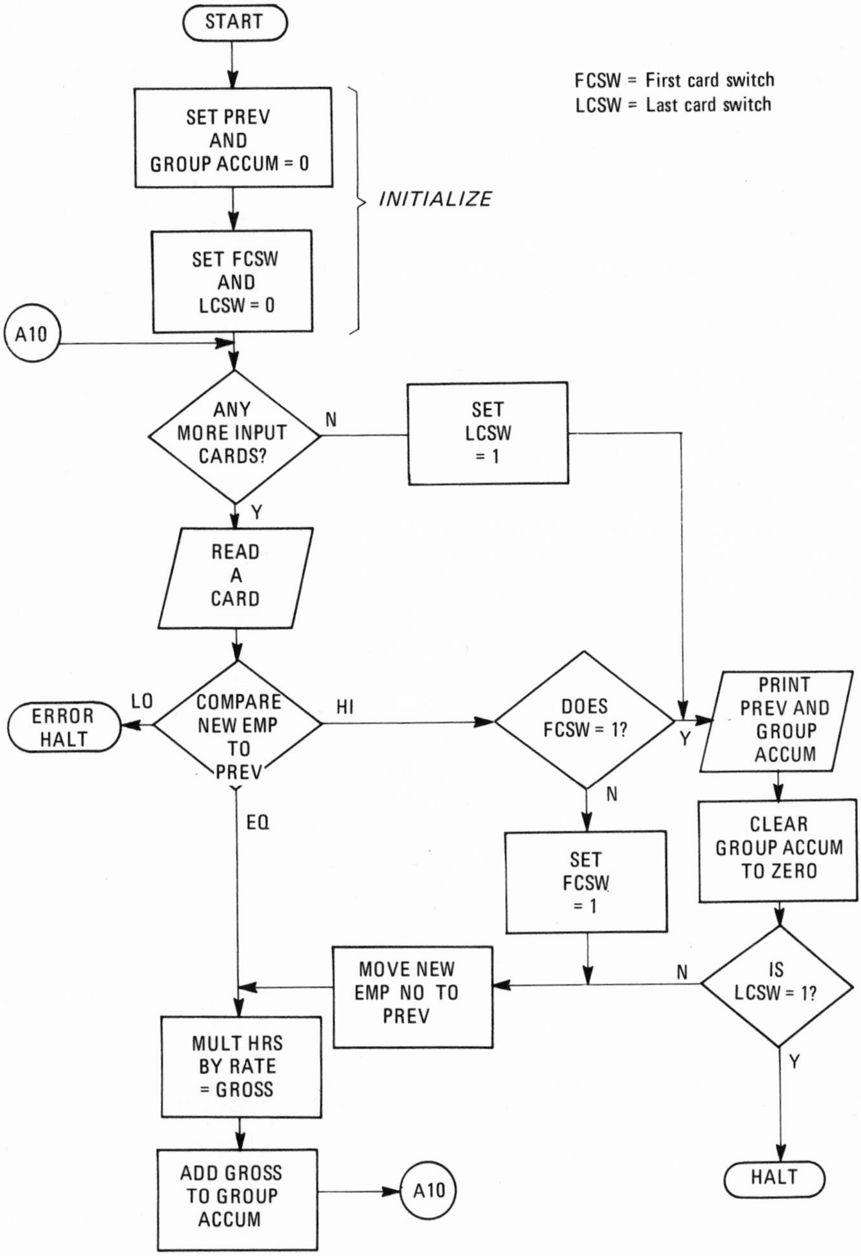

Fig. 3-4. Simple Control Break Using Switches.

Switches can be very useful when used in moderation. However, *the use of numerous switches in a program can make it very confusing and difficult to follow and should be avoided if possible.*

SOLUTION WITHOUT SWITCHES

Figure 3-5 shows the same problem solved without the use of switches. In the case of the first card we make use of the fact, already noted, that when this card is read the previous control number is zero. A branch can therefore be initiated by an appropriate compare instruction rather than by testing a switch. (We are assuming that no input card has a control number of zero.)

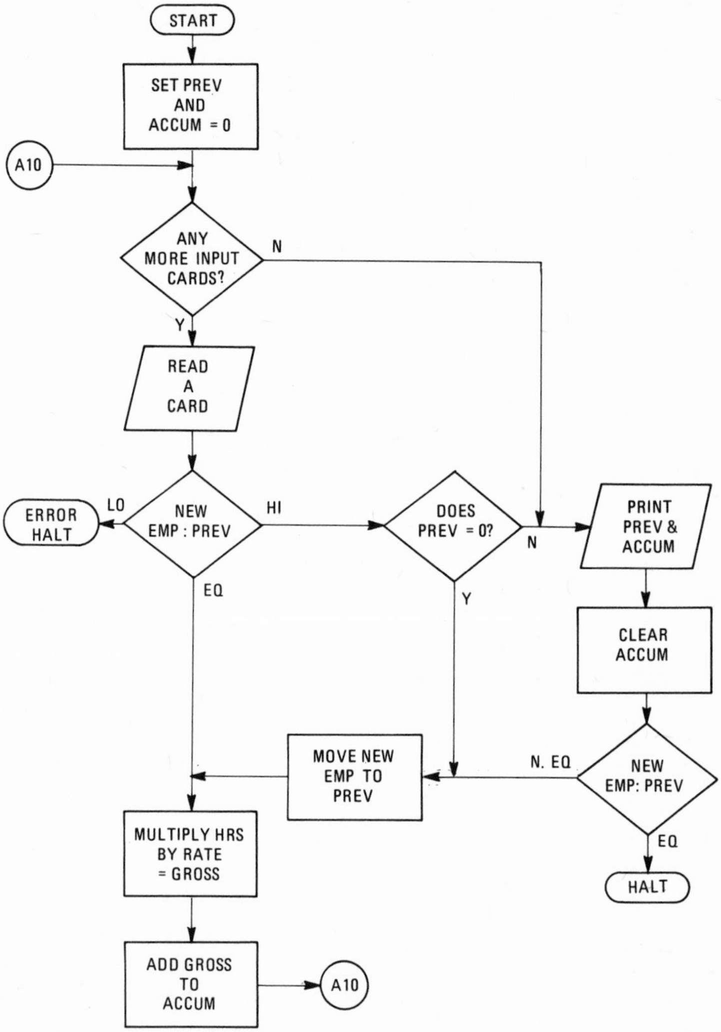

Fig. 3-5. Simple Control Break (No Switches Required).

In the case of the last card, we note that normally when we have just completed the output routine, on a control break, it is because we have a new employee number higher than the previous employee number. In the case where we have branched to the output routine from the last card test, however, the two employee numbers are equal. This can be used in an appropriate compare instruction to branch out of the normal control break routine into the final end of job routine.

There are many variations of this simple control break. In most of them final grand totals will be required at the end of the job. In some of them there may be more than one kind of card in each group. Problem 3-1 (at the end of this chapter) may now be attempted.

FILES

Up to this point we have considered problems involving only one type of card. In these cases the entire *file* of cards consists of this one type of card. Commonly, however, in business problems the solution requires two or more distinct types of cards in the computer run. Quite often the different types of cards will consist of the following:

Master Cards

These are cards containing data that are permanent or semipermanent in nature. They are generally identified by a specific card number in some column. For example, an inventory master card may be identified by a card code 1. It may contain permanent information such as stock number, stock description, and price. It may also contain semipermanent data such as quantity on hand, value on hand, and date.

Transaction or Detail Cards

These are cards of a temporary nature. They generally contain data for the current period, say the current week or month. For example, transactions for the current period involving receipts of inventory stock will be keypunched on transaction cards. The card will contain a unique card code such as a 2. It may also in this case contain stock number, quantity received, value of receipt, and date of receipt.

FILE UPDATING

At some point, say at the end of the week or month, it is necessary to apply the current transactions to the permanent master records. The two files must be sorted or merged together according to the control field. The combined file will now be in ascending sequence of control field with the master card ahead of the transaction cards for each unique control field.

For example, if we combine the inventory receipt cards with the inventory master cards according to stock number, we will get for the first stock number a master card followed by the receipts for the current period for that stock. Next will appear the master card for the second stock number followed by its receipts cards.

It is important to know here that:

1. There will normally be one only master card for each stock number; and
2. There may be normally any number of receipt cards. There may be none or there may be many.

For the programmer the problem is to ensure that, for each unique stock number in the file, there is one master card and that it is the first card for each stock number group. We must also provide in the program for the possibility that there may be missing master cards. These are error conditions for which suitable programming action must be taken.

Example 3-1 illustrates this type of application.

EXAMPLE 3-1

Inventory Control Break

A computer is to be used to calculate current inventory value by item number, producing a report showing

Item Number Quantity Value

–one line per item with grand totals at the end.

INPUT:

A deck of cards sorted by item number, each new item number being preceded by a master card containing the current price per unit. There must be one and only one master card for each item number, but there may be any number of detail cards. Figure 3-6 shows the format of the input deck.

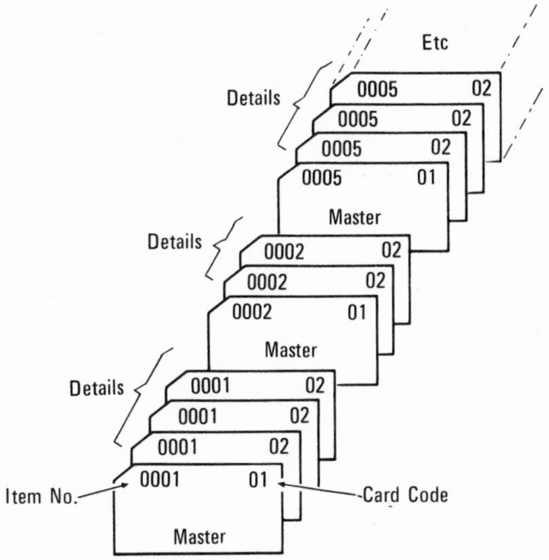

Note: Price on the master cards and quantity on the detail cards are not shown.

Fig. 3-6. Typical Input Deck for Example 3-1.

	DATA	*CARD COLUMNS*
Master card	Item number	1-4
	Price XXX.XX	5-9
	Card code 01	79-80
Detail card	Item number	1-4
	Quantity XXX	10-12
	Card code 02	79-80

SOLUTION: Figure 3-7 shows the flowchart.

NOTES:

1. E10, E20, and E30 are suitable error routines terminating in either a halt or a return to the last card test.
2. ITEM, QUANT, and INPRICE refer to data in the input area. PREV and STOREDPRICE refer to data from the master card stored in some area other than the input area.
3. QUANTACCUM and VALACCUM accumulate totals for each item and are cleared and reused as the item number changes.
4. TOTNO and TOTVAL accumulate final totals of all items.

The PLC coding follows.

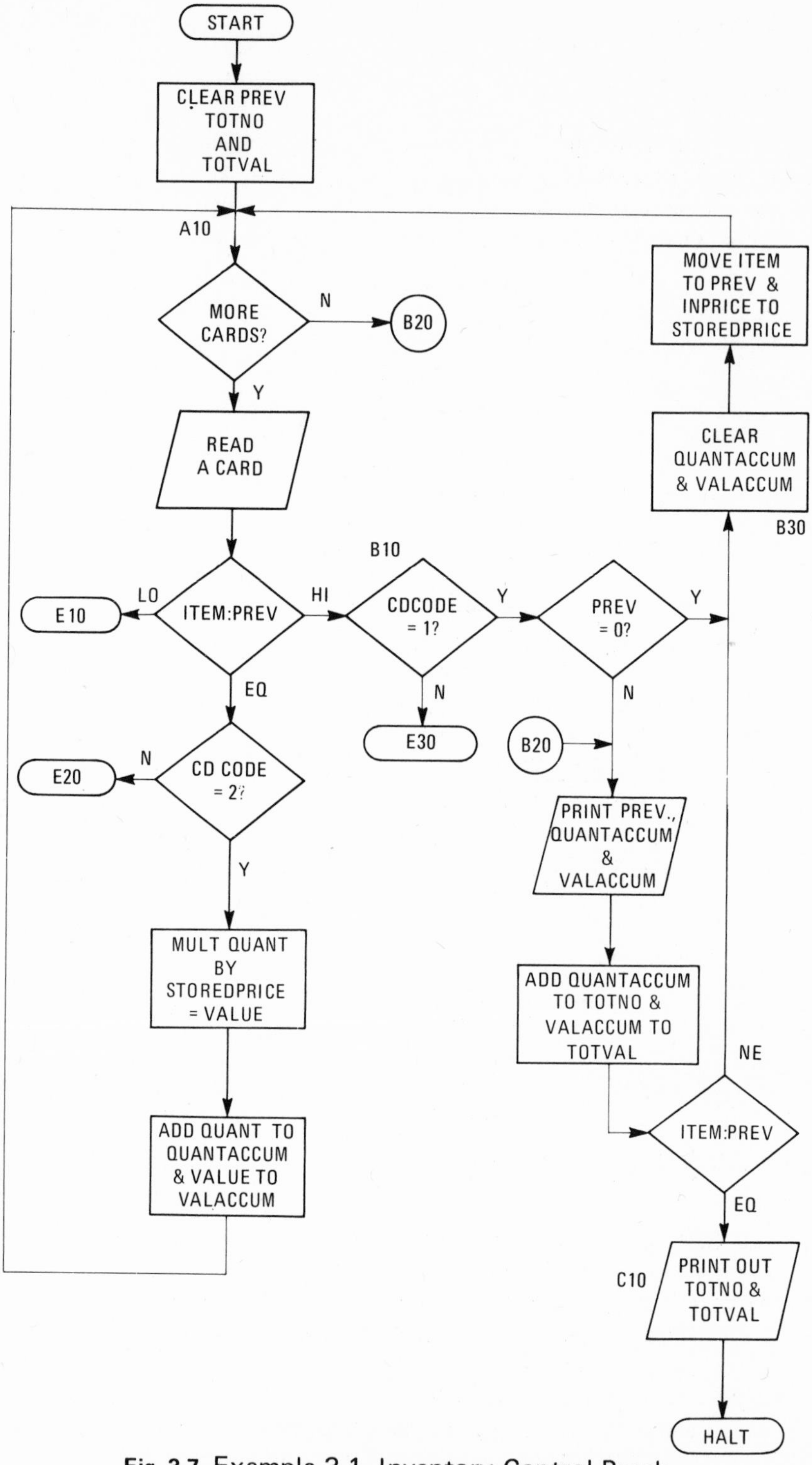

Fig. 3-7. Example 3-1, Inventory Control Break.

PLC Coding for Example 3-1

LABEL	*OPERATION*	*OPERANDS*	*COMMENTS*
START	CLEAR	PREV	Initializing
	CLEAR	TOTNO	
	CLEAR	TOTVAL	
A10	BLC	TO B20	
	READ CARD	INTO INPUT	
	COMPARE	ITEM TO PREV	
	BL	TO E10	Sequence error
	BH	TO B10	Control break
	COMPARE	CDCODE TO '2'	
	BNE	TO E20	
	MULT	QUANT BY STOREDPRICE	This gives VALUE
	ADD	QUANT TO QUANTACCUM	
	ADD	VALUE TO VALACCUM	
	B	TO A10	Conclusion of processing of detail cards
B10	COMPARE	CDCODE TO '1'	Start of control break routine
	BNE	TO E30	
	COMPARE	PREV TO '0'	First card test
	BE	TO B30	
B20	MOVE	PREV TO PREVOUT	
	MOVE	QUANTACCUM TO QUANTOUT	
	MOVE	VALACCUM TO VALOUT	
	PRINT LINE	FROM OUTPUT	
	ADD	QUANTACCUM TO TOTNO	} Accumulating final totals
	ADD	VALACCUM TO TOTVAL	

PLC Coding for Example 3-1 (Continued)

LABEL	*OPERATION*	*OPERANDS*	*COMMENTS*
	COMPARE	ITEM TO PREV	Last card test
	BE	TO C10	
B30	CLEAR	QUANTACCUM	Preparing for next control group
	CLEAR	VALACCUM	
	MOVE	ITEM TO PREV	
	MOVE	INPRICE TO STOREDPRICE	
	B	TO A10	
C10	MOVE	TOTNO TO QUANTOUT	Final totals printout
	MOVE	TOTVAL TO VALOUT	
	PRINT LINE	FROM OUTPUT	
	HALT		End of job
E10	MOVE	'SEQUENCE ERROR' TO OUTPUT	
	B	TO E40	
E20	MOVE	'INVALID DETAIL' TO OUTPUT	
	B	TO E40	
E30	MOVE	'INVALID MASTER' TO OUTPUT	
E40	PRINT LINE	FROM OUTPUT	
	HALT		Error halt
INPUT	DEFINE	80	Declaratives

PLC Coding for Example 3-1 (Continued)

LABEL	*OPERATION*	*OPERANDS*	*COMMENTS*
ITEM	DEFINE	INPUT (1-4)	
INPRICE	DEFINE	INPUT (5-9)	
QUANT	DEFINE	INPUT (10-12)	
CDCODE	DEFINE	INPUT (79-80)	
OUTPUT	DEFINE	120	
PREV-OUT	DEFINE	OUTPUT (1-4)	
QUANT-OUT	DEFINE	OUTPUT (10-15)	
VALOUT	DEFINE	OUTPUT (20-29)	
QUANT-ACCUM	DEFINE	5	
VAL-ACCUM	DEFINE	9	
TOTNO	DEFINE	6	
TOTVAL	DEFINE	10	
STORED-PRICE	DEFINE	5	
PREV	DEFINE	4	
VALUE	DEFINE	8	Product area
	END		

PROBLEMS

PROBLEM 3-1 (mandatory)

Purchase Analysis

At the end of each month a company wishes to analyze its purchases by general ledger account number. To do this it sorts purchase distribution cards into general ledger account number order and then feeds them into a computer. For each account number, a summary card is punched out, and at the end of the run a control total card is punched.

INPUT

Distribution cards sorted into general ledger number order:

	COLUMNS
Account number	1-5
Amount	6-12

There may be any number of cards for each account. Input cards should be sequence checked.

OUTPUT

One card per account:

	COLUMNS
Account number	1-5
Amount	6-15

plus a card with a grand total of all accounts at the end of the run: columns 1-12.

PROBLEM 3-2 (mandatory)

Updating Department Store Accounts Receivable

OBJECTIVE

To apply charges (sales) and credits (payments) to each customer's master charge account on punched cards.

SOURCE DATA

Punched cards

MASTER CARD (01)		*SALES CARD (02)*		*PAYMENT CARD (03)*	
	Columns		Columns		Columns
Card code (01)	1-2	Card code (02)	1-2	Card code (03)	1-2
Account Number	3-6	Account Number	3-6	Account Number	3-6

Name	11-30				
Balance	34-40	Amount	34-40	Amount	34-40
Credit limit	44-50				
Month	79-80	Month	79-80	Month	79-80

NOTE WELL: Credit (X), if any, is punched in column 40. Because of reversing or correcting entries, any card may contain a credit. Payment cards normally contain an X punch, so they are to be added to the balance.

PROCEDURE

1. Sequence check the card input by account number.
2. There must be *one* master card for each account, and it must be the first card.
3. There may be *any* number of sales or payment cards for an account.
4. Punch out in the same format a new updated master card for each account.
5. If the new balance exceeds the "limit," punch a 1 in column 70 of the new master card; otherwise, leave the column blank.
6. Update the month on the new updated master card by incrementing the month in the old master card.

REQUIRED

1. Program flowchart
2. Documentation
3. Program—assembled and tested

HINTS

1. Remember that last month's master may have a 1 in column 70.
2. Updating December's master cards will require special treatment.

PROBLEM 3-3 (mandatory)

Updating an Inventory File

REQUIRED: Flowchart only.

INPUT

		CONTAINS
Card code 1	Description card	Stock number, description
Card code 2	Balance forward	Stock number, balance forward, month
Card code 3	Receipts	Stock number, receipt quantity, month
Card code 4	Issues	Stock number, issue quantity, month

OUTPUT

New balance forward card code 2.

PROCEDURE

1. Read in a date card (card code 99) and store the date.
2. Ensure that there is *only one* card code 1 and *only one* card code 2 for each stock number. There may be any number of cards code 3 and 4.
3. Check that all input cards contain a valid month, i.e., that cards code 3 and 4 agree with the date card, and that card code 2 is one month prior.
4. Punch a new updated balance forward card containing current month.
5. Provide final totals of old balances, receipts, issues, and new balances.

4

Multilevel Control Breaks

MINOR, INTERMEDIATE, AND MAJOR TOTALS

We have seen in our study of the simple or single-level control break how we can obtain one level of subtotals. Very often reports are required in which several levels of subtotals are required. This can best be understood by a study of the illustration of such a report in Figure 4-1.

In this example, products (with a two-digit code number) are sold by a store with several branches (indicated by a two-digit code number) in several cities (indicated by a one-digit code number). There is an input card for each sale and all the cards are printed, as well as various totals.

The following features of such a report should be noted and fully understood.

1. Within each city, and within each branch in each city, totals are required for each product. These are called the *minor* totals. The same product sold

by a different branch will have a separate total (e.g., product 21 sold by branches 11 and 12 in city 1).

2. It follows that whenever any one of the three control fields (city, branch, or product) changes, a printout of the minor total product accumulator must occur. This applies even though the next product may be the same (e.g., product 6 sold by branches 4 and 5 in city 2)
3. Similarly, a change of city will cause a printout of both branch and product accumulators. Branch is called the *intermediate* control field, and city is the *major control* field.
4. We have the rule, therefore, that a higher-level control break will cause all lower-level control breaks to occur.

Sales Analysis By Product, Branch, and City

CITY	*BRANCH*	*PRODUCT*	*AMOUNT*
1	11	21	100.00
1	11	21	75.00
1	11	21	30.00
		(PRODUCT TOTAL)	205.00 *
1	11	22	150.00
1	11	22	20.00
		(PRODUCT TOTAL)	170.00 *
		(BRANCH TOTAL)	375.00 **
1	12	13	80.00
1	12	13	100.00
		(PRODUCT TOTAL)	180.00 *
1	12	21	50.00
1	12	21	60.00
		(PRODUCT TOTAL)	110.00 *
		(BRANCH TOTAL)	290.00 **
		(CITY TOTAL)	665.00 ***
2	04	06	10.00
2	04	06	30.00
		(PRODUCT TOTAL)	40.00 *
		(BRANCH TOTAL)	40.00 **
2	05	06	25.00
2	05	06	17.00
	.		
	.		
	.		

Fig. 4-1. Detail Listing with Totals.

5. When a total is printed, the accumulator must be added into the accumulator for the next higher level total and then cleared. (This is called "rolling" the total.)
6. Totals must be computed and printed out, starting with the lowest level and proceeding to higher levels in turn.
7. In the illustration given, every input card is printed in full. This is known as a *detail listing.* In other cases, the indicative information (city, branch, product) might be printed only when a change in that field occurs. This makes the report a little less cluttered and easier to read (see Figure 4-2). This is known as *group indication.*

Sales Analysis By Product, Branch, and City

CITY	*BRANCH*	*PRODUCT*	*AMOUNT*
1	11	21	100.00
			75.00
			30.00
		(PRODUCT TOTAL)	205.00 *
		22	150.00
			20.00
		(PRODUCT TOTAL)	170.00 *
		(BRANCH TOTAL)	375.00 **
	12	13	80.00
			100.00
		(PRODUCT TOTAL)	180.00 *
		21	50.00
			60.00
		(PRODUCT TOTAL)	110.00 *
		(BRANCH TOTAL)	290.00 **
		(CITY TOTAL)	665.00 ***
2	04	06	10.00
			30.00
		(PRODUCT TOTAL)	40.00 *
		(BRANCH TOTAL)	40.00 **
	05	06	25.00
			17.00
		.	
		.	
		.	

Fig. 4-2. Detail Listing with Group Indication.

Alternatively, every input card might not be printed, but only the indicative information and the totals (see Figure 4-3). This is known as a *tabulation* of group totals by city, branch, and product.

When all the detail must be printed, an even clearer report can be obtained, if space permits, by offsetting the totals as in Figure 4-4.

Sales Analysis By Product, Branch, and City

CITY	*BRANCH*	*PRODUCT*	*AMOUNT*
1	11	21	205.00 *
1	11	22	170.00 *
			375.00 **
1	12	13	180.00 *
1	12	21	110.00 *
			290.00 **
			665.00 ***
2	04	06	40.00 *
			40.00 **
2	05	06	

.
.
.

Fig. 4-3. Tabulation with Group Totals.

8. Note the use of asterisks to indicate the different levels of total:

*	for the lowest level (minor)
**	for the next higher level (intermediate)
***	for the next higher level (major), and so on.

A print position is left between the amount and the asterisk for printing minus signs. Two positions are required if CR is to be printed.

CHECKING THE SEQUENCE

First notice the sequence of the cards. These are arranged so that we can obtain totals for each product in each branch, totals for each

Sales Analysis By Product, Branch, and City

CITY	BRANCH	PRODUCT	AMOUNT	TOTALS BY PRODUCT	BRANCH	CITY
1	11	21	100.00			
1	11	21	75.00			
1	11	21	30.00			
				205.00 *		
1	11	22	150.00			
1	11	22	20.00			
				170.00 *	375.00 **	
1	12	13	80.00			
1	12	13	100.00			
				180.00 *		
1	12	21	50.00			
1	12	21	60.00			
				110.00 *	290.00 **	665.00 ***
2	04	06	10.00			
2	04	06	30.00			
				40.00 *	40.00 **	
2	05	06	25.00			
2	05	06	17.00			
	.					
	.					
	.					

Fig. 4-4. Detail Listing with Offset Totals

branch in each city, and totals for each city. There will, of course, also be a final grand total.

How can we check that this sequence is correct?

The product number is not necessarily in increasing sequence and neither is the branch number.

We shall consider two of the many possible approaches to this problem. A third method will be covered in Chapter 9.

SOLUTION USING SWITCHES (SEE FIGURE 4-5)

In this method, we check for a change in any of the three control field numbers starting with the major field (city), followed by the intermediate field (branch), and then the minor field (product). If any control field has decreased after higher-level fields have been found equal, we have a sequence error.

If any control field has increased, no further checks of lower-level control fields are necessary since we must automatically activate control breaks at their levels. This automatically avoids the difficulty that an increase in control field at one level may be accompanied by a decrease at a lower level.

Instead, we turn on a switch to record the fact that this particular level of control break has occurred. We can then proceed to print out totals starting at the lowest level and to use the state of the switches to decide at which level to stop printing totals. Each switch should be a core position uniquely labeled, such as BRSW for branch switch. If it contains a zero it is off, if a one it is on.

Let us follow through the main steps of the flowchart in Figure 4-5 using the sample data shown in Figure 4-1.

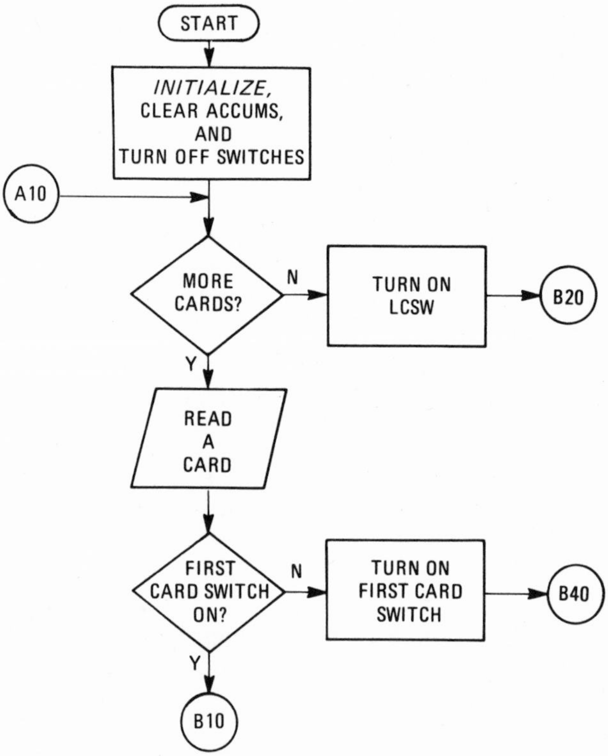

Fig. 4-5. Three-level Control Break Using Switches.

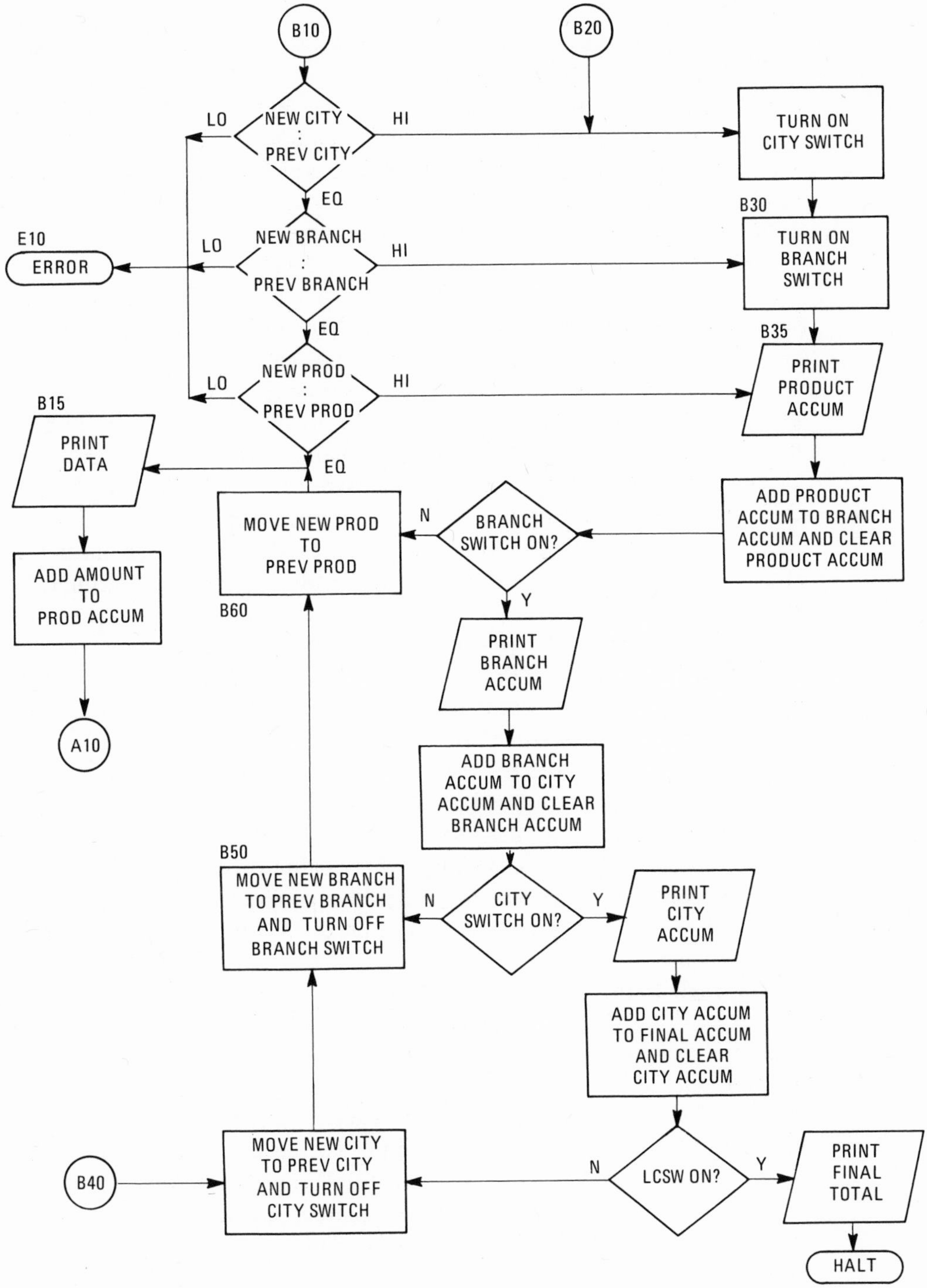

Fig. 4-5. Continued.

After initializing and testing for the last card, we read the first card for city 1, branch 11, and product 21. Since the first card switch is not on, it is turned on and we bypass the control break routines to B40 where the control field numbers 1, 11, and 21 are stored in PREV CITY, PREV BRANCH, and PREV PROD. The data in the card are printed on the first line of the report, the amount is accumulated, and we return to the beginning, A10.

The next card has the same control field values so we pass straight through the three control break comparisons on equal, print the data, accumulate the amount, and return again to A10.

The same procedure is used for the third card.

The fourth card has the same city and branch but a different product number, 22. At the third control break comparison it therefore compares high. This tells us that we have already processed *all* the cards of the previous product. We now suspend processing of this fourth card, holding its data in the input area, while we print out the total of product 21, add this total to the branch accumulator, and clear the product accumulator, ready to start accumulating amounts for product 22.

At this point the BRANCH switch is not on, so we now replace the value 21 in PREV PROD with the value 22. We are now at B15, having completed the control break, and so we can return to the fourth card, which is still sitting in the input area, and process it by printing and accumulating.

The fifth card is processed as an "equal" to the fourth card.

We come now to the sixth card. On this card the city is unchanged, but the branch is high whereas the product is low. This is perfectly valid and we see that the low product sequence will not cause a low sequence error since the product comparison is bypassed by the high branch compare.

The high branch compare tells us that we must suspend processing of the sixth card and print out totals of branch 11. However, we must not forget that we must first compute and print out the total of product 22, so in order to remind us later that we require a branch total we turn on the branch switch. Then, after printing out product 22 total, a test of the branch switch tells us that a branch total is also required. The branch total routine is similar to the product total routine. When it is completed, including the storing of the new branch 12 in PREVBRANCH in place of the old 11, we can proceed with the processing of the sixth card.

The procedure is similar for a change in city, as on the tenth card, and in fact the process can be extended to as many levels of total as are required.

As with the simple control break, we must not forget that after the last card has been processed we must print out totals at all three levels. A branch to B20 takes care of this and a subsequent test of switch LCSW (turned on before branching to B20) permits the break out from the normal routine to the final total printout routine at the end of the job.

The PLC coding of the control break routines might be

LABEL	*OPERATION*	*OPERANDS*	*COMMENTS*
B10	COMPARE	NEWCITY TO PREVCITY	
	BL	TO E10	Sequence error routine
	BH	TO B20	City control break
	COMPARE	NEWBRANCH TO PREVBRANCH	
	BL	TO E10	
	BH	TO B30	Branch control break
	COMPARE	NEWPROD TO PREVPROD	
	BL	TO E10	
	BH	TO B35	Product control break
B15	PRINT LINE	INPUT DATA	
	ADD	AMOUNT TO PRODACCUM	
	B	TO A10	
B20	MOVE	'1' TO CITYSWITCH	Turn on appropriate switches
B30	MOVE	'1' TO BRANCHSWITCH	
B35	PRINT LINE	PRODACCUM	
	ADD	PRODACCUM TO BRANCHACCUM	
	CLEAR	PRODACCUM	

(Continued)

LABEL	OPERATION	OPERANDS	COMMENTS
	COMPARE	BRANCHSWITCH TO '1'	
	BNE	TO B60	
	PRINT LINE	BRANCHACCUM	Branch total routine
	ADD	BRANCHACCUM TO CITYACCUM	
	CLEAR	BRANCHACCUM	
	COMPARE	CITYSWITCH TO '1'	
	BNE	TO B50	
	PRINT LINE	CITYACCUM	City total routine
	ADD	CITYACCUM TO FINALACCUM	
	CLEAR	CITYACCUM	
	COMPARE	LCSW TO '1'	
	BE	To final total routine	
B40	MOVE	NEWCITY TO PREVCITY	
	MOVE	'0' TO CITYSWITCH	
B50	MOVE	NEWBRANCH TO PREVBRANCH	
	MOVE	'0' TO BRANCHSWITCH	
B60	MOVE	NEWPROD TO PREVPROD	
	B	TO B15	
Final total routine follows from this point			

SOLUTION AVOIDING SWITCHES—CONTROL WORD APPROACH

If we consider for the moment only city 1 in the example given, we have the following sequence of numbers representing branch and product:

11 21
11 21
11 21
11 22
11 22
12 13
12 13
12 21
12 21

As pointed out earlier, the product number is not in increasing sequence. However, if we consider each line as one four-digit number, these numbers are in increasing sequence. Hence our test for sequence can be made on a field made up of the two fields "branch" and "product" combined. We will refer to the combined control word field as the "BRPROD field."

Printing the Totals

If the new control field (on the card just read in) is higher than the previous control field, we must suspend reading cards and print out a product total. This applies even though the product number may not have changed–only the branch number may have changed (see the eleventh and twelfth case of cards shown in Figure 4-1).

The first comparison (NEW BRPROD : PREV BRPROD) shown in Figure 4-6 followed by a printout of the product total in the case of a high comparison shows how this is done.

If the high comparison was due, in whole or in part, to a change in branch number rather than merely a change in product number, we must next print out a branch total. To check this, the printout of product total is followed by a comparison on the branch field only (NEW BRANCH : PREV BRANCH) instead of on the combined field.

If the comparison is high, then a branch total is printed out. If not, a branch total is not required. In both cases the new control fields are copied into the previous control fields ready for the next card, and processing is resumed.

Thus with the sequence of numbers shown above, the change of BRPROD from 1121 to 1122 will first cause a printout of the product total. The subsequent check on BRANCH only (i.e., 11) indicates no change in branch number and so there will be no further printout at this point.

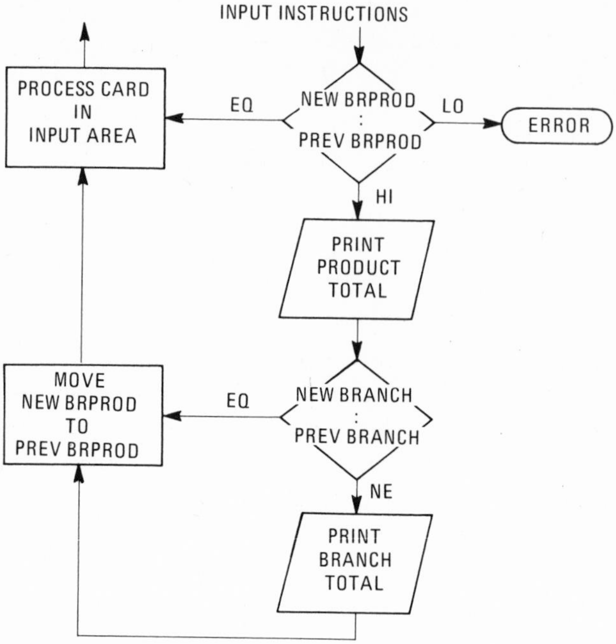

Fig. 4-6. Basic Multilevel Control Break Avoiding Switches.

Later, when the first card for branch 12 is read in (1213), the change in BRPROD from 1122 to 1213 will again cause a printout of the product total. This time, however, the subsequent check, on BRANCH only, will show a change (from 11 to 12). A branch total printout will, therefore, be initiated.

THE COMPLETE FLOWCHART

The extension of this principle to the complete flowchart using a control word made up of the three fields "city," "branch," and "product" as shown in Figure 4-7 should now be clear.

The following comments may be of assistance.

1. The technique used in the simple control break for the last card routine will not work here, since on the last card we must force printout of all levels of total. Instead, the technique of changing the new CITYBRPROD field to all 9's is used. This is neater and more efficient than the other

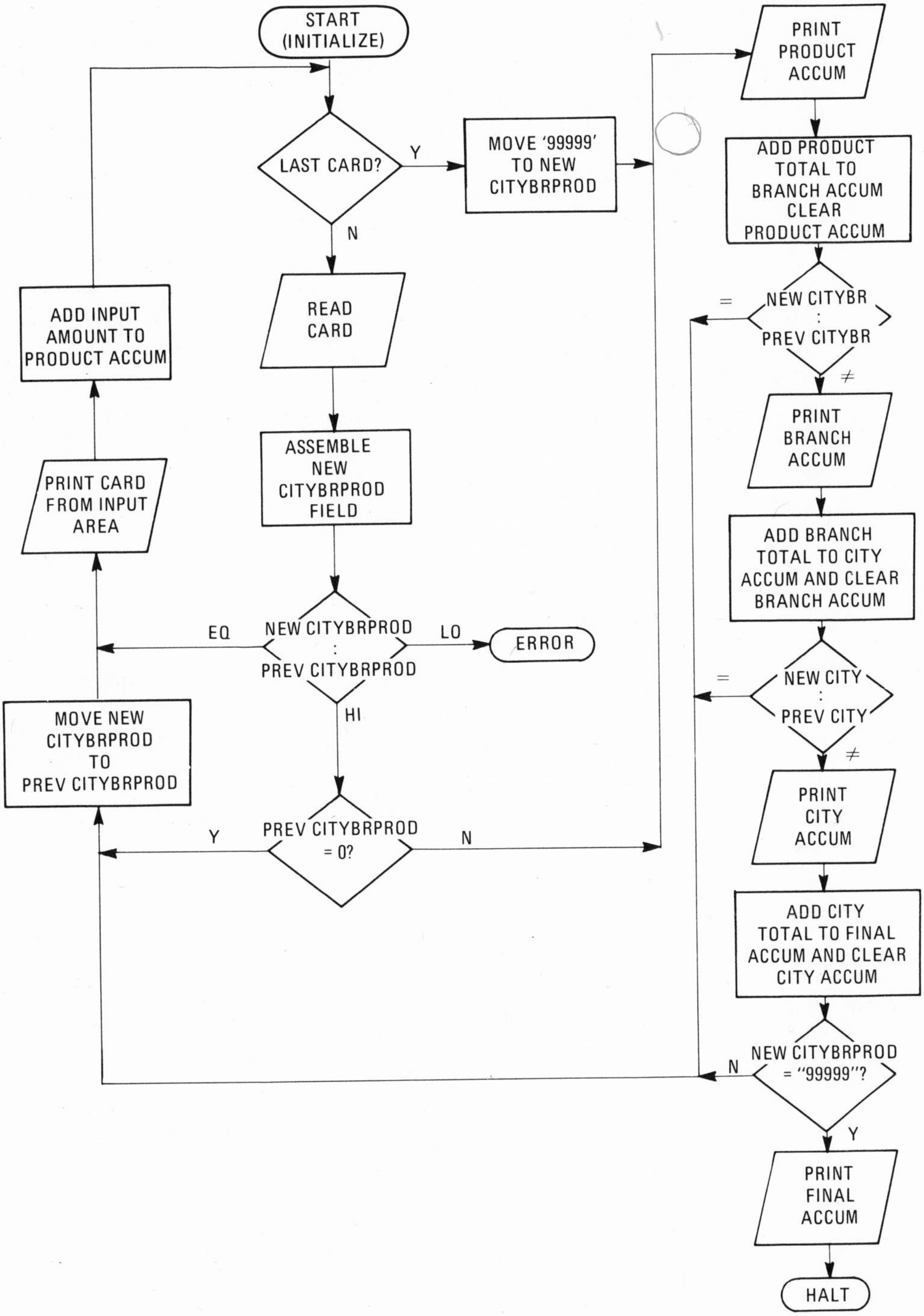

Fig. 4-7. Three-level Control Break Without Switches.

alternative of setting a switch. *Note:* This technique assumes there is no valid CITYBRPROD equal to all 9's. Otherwise all zeros may be used. In 360 Assembler language, hexadecimal F's may be used.

2. The standard first card test is used.
3. As each total is printed, it is added to the accumulator for the next highest level of total. The accumulator just printed out is then cleared, ready for the next batch of amounts to be added into it.

The solution using a control word for multi level control breaks is superior to the use of switches. It makes little difference whether there are two, three, four or more control levels. The logical structure of the flowchart will remain the same. If there are more levels, it is necessary only to extend the control word and to provide additional comparisons and totals.

PROBLEMS

PROBLEM 4-1 (mandatory)

Extension and Totals of Employee Time Cards

INPUT

	COLUMNS
Card code (22)	1-2
Store number	3-4
Department number	5-7
Employee number	8-11
Employee name	13-33
Month	34-35
Job number	38-40
Hours (XX.X)	41-43
Rate (X.XXX)	44-47

PROCEDURE

1. Sequence check input according to minor: employee number (any number of cards per employee); intermediate: department; and major: store.
2. Print *detail* for each employee including the extended pay (hours × rate), rounded to the nearest cent.
3. Print *total* hours and pay for each employee, each department, each store, and the final total.

OUTPUT

A report similar to the following:

STORE	*DEPT.*	*EMP. NO.*	*NAME*	*HRS*	*RATE*	*PAY*
01	003	0163	FR SMITH	20.0	1.250	25.00
01	003	0163	FR SMITH	15.0	1.500	22.50
				35.0 *		47.50 *

REQUIRED

Get the program to work and prepare full documentation including object listing, list of test data with proof of calculations, test output, flowchart, and program description.

PROBLEM 4-2 (mandatory)

Sales Analysis

REQUIRED
Flowchart only.

INPUT

Card code 31. Salesman master card; contains division, district number, salesman number, and name (one card per salesman)

Card code 32. Sales detail card; contains division, district number, salesman number, product number, amount sold, and month (any number of details per product per salesman)

OUTPUT
Report of the following format:

DIVISION	*DISTRICT*	*SALESMAN*	*NAME*	*PRODUCT*	*AMOUNT*
01	06	023	J M DOAKS	015	100.00
01	06	023	J M DOAKS	018	50.00
01	06	023	J M DOAKS	033	100.00
					250.00 *

.
.
.

Sequence check and provide totals by

Minor	product number
Intermediate	salesman
Major	district
Major major	division
Final total	

Check for valid card codes and month.

5

Arithmetic Considerations

Most commercial computer programs involve some arithmetic operations. In many cases these include only addition, subtraction, and comparison.

ADDITION AND SUBTRACTION

The main problem that arises under these conditions is that of ensuring that the fields set up in the memory for the accumulation and storage of answers are long enough to accommodate the largest possible answers that are expected to occur. Consideration should be given here not only to present conditions but also to those that might arise through growth or other changes in the business.

A second problem may arise whenever subtraction occurs. The answer *may* turn out to be negative. This may or may not be permissible, depending on the problem. If it is not permissible, appropriate action must be provided.

EXAMPLE 5-1

Calculation of Income Tax

An employee's taxable income is equal to gross pay minus exemptions. If in a certain period his gross pay is very small because of sickness, layoff, etc., it may be smaller than his exemption, resulting in a negative taxable income. Obviously in such a case it may be necessary that the normal procedure for calculating tax be bypassed.

When multiplication and division are included in a program, other problems arise. These will be discussed from the viewpoint of an assembler-type language, since many of them are taken care of automatically in higher-level languages such as Cobol, Fortran, or PL/I.

ROUNDING OFF OR HALF-ADJUSTING

The result of a multiplication or division may include more decimal places than are required in the final answer (e.g., tenths of a cent). Generally, these unwanted decimals are not merely dropped (truncated) but must be examined to determine whether the last decimal figure to be kept should be increased by 1 or not, e.g.,

$1.754 would give $1.75 when rounded

$1.756 would give $1.76 when rounded.

A simple method of programming this is to add 5 to the digit to be eliminated. Make the resultant carry (if any). Then eliminate the digit in the unwanted position. The carry, if any, will take care of the rounding, e.g.,

	1.754	1.756
Add:	5	5
	1.759	1.761
Answer:	1.75	1.76

If more than one digit is to be eliminated, the 5 is added to the leftmost one that is to be eliminated:

	1.7546	1.7562
Add:	5	5
	1.7596	1.7612
Answer:	1.75	1.76

Rounding Off Negative Numbers

If the answer can possibly be negative, additional provision must be made to detect this, since the 5 must then be *subtracted* instead of added. A test for a negative answer and a branch to a routine to subtract 5 instead of adding can be used.

In some cases a slightly different technique can be used to take care of both positive and negative answers with no special testing. This applies where the right-hand end of the amount field contains the sign (e.g., packed format on the I.B.M. 360 computer). In this case instead of adding 5 to the digits to be dropped, the digit itself (including the sign) is added. If the sign is negative, the digit will be automatically subtracted. The following examples will illustrate this method:

	1.754+	1.756+	1.756–
Add:	4+	6+	6–
	1.758+	1.762+	1.762–
Answer:	1.75	1.76	-1.76
	1.75432+	1.75632+	1.75632–
Add:	432+	632+	632–
	1.75864+	1.76264+	1.76264–
Answer:	1.75	1.76	-1.76

MULTIPLICATION

Two major considerations arise in multiplication: total number of digits in the product and number of decimal places.

Total Number of Digits

When two numbers are multiplied, the number of digits in the product will depend on the magnitude of the two numbers. When we are writing a program, we do not know what the values of the numbers are going to be, but because of their field lengths we do know the range of *possible* values. In particular, we must know the maximum values so that we can assign data fields large enough to accommodate them. Obviously, we will obtain the largest sized product when we multiply together the two largest values the data fields can accommodate, i.e., all 9's, e.g.,

999	three digits
× 99	two digits
8991	
8991	
98901	five digits

A few trials should soon convince the reader that under these conditions we have the following rule.

Rule

The maximum length of the product (number of digits) is equal to the sum of the lengths of the two numbers being multiplied (multiplicand and multiplier).

In designing the program, then, we are safe if we follow this rule even though we may know that the answer, with practical values, may not be this large. If the product is shorter than the maximum length, the left-hand end of the answer area will be filled out with leading zeros.

EXAMPLE 5-2

Quantity A:	defined as a four-digit field	0 1 2 7
Quantity B:	defined as a two-digit field	1 2
Product A × B:	defined as a six digit field	0 0 1 5 2 4

It must be clearly understood that in computer arithmetic it is the *defined* lengths of the fields being multiplied that determine the length of the product field, not the actual values. Thus in Example 5-2, if A were 0001 and B were 02, the product would still be a six-digit field, 000002.

Number of Decimal Places

In doing arithmetic, the computer treats all numbers as integers. Therefore, when working with decimal fractions (in an assembler-type language) *we must keep track of the decimal point ourselves.* Fortunately, we again have a simple rule which the reader can verify by a few trial calculations.

Rule

The number of decimal places in the product is equal to the sum of the number of decimal places in the multiplicand and multiplier.

EXAMPLE 5-3

99.9	three digits, one decimal place
X 9.9	two digits, one decimal place
89.91	
899.1	
989.01	five digits, two decimal places

EXAMPLE 5-4

Quantity A:	four-digit field with two decimals, i.e., of form XX.XX	0 1 ∧ 2 7
Quantity B:	two-digit field with two decimals, i.e., of form .XX	∧ 1 2
Product A X B:	six-digit field with four decimals	0 0 ∧ 1 5 2 4

NOTE: The sign ∧ is used to indicate the position of the implied decimal point.

Notice that the program can be designed without consideration of actual numbers by using the two rules given above and representation of digits by X's. It is recommended that this technique be adopted. It involves no arithmetic calculations and covers all possible cases.

Thus Example 5-4 would be solved as follows:

Multiplicand field:	XX.XX
Multiplier field:	.XX
Product field:	XX.XXXX

Other examples would be:

X.X	X.XXX
X.X	XX
XX.XX	XXX.XXX

DIVISION

Division can be more confusing than multiplication, but again there are a few simple rules which ensure satisfactory results in all cases.

Terminology

The terminology of division is explained by the following equation:

$$\frac{\text{DIVIDEND}}{\text{DIVISOR}} = \text{QUOTIENT} + \text{REMAINDER}$$

The first principle to be grasped is that the computer works only with integers. Therefore, the programmer must make all necessary allowances for decimal places when working in an assembler-type language. From this principle, which means that the smallest possible valid divisor is 1, follows the first rule.

Rule

The largest possible number of digits in the quotient is the same as the number of digits in the dividend.

Consider now the following divisions:

$$\frac{99.99}{3} = 33.33$$

$$\frac{9999}{3} = 3333$$

$$\frac{9.999}{0.3} = 33.33$$

$$\frac{9.999}{3} = 3.333$$

These are all calculated by the computer as

$$\frac{9999}{3} = 3333$$

How, then, can we establish the position of the decimal point? One simple method is to mentally eliminate the decimals in the divisor by multiplying both dividend and divisor by a suitable power of 10. The number of decimals in the quotient will then be equal to the number in the dividend; e.g.,

$$\frac{9.999}{0.3} = \frac{99.99}{3}$$

if numerator and denominator are multiplied by 10. Hence there are two decimals in the quotient.

Another method is to use the rule that follows.

Rule

The number of decimal places in the quotient is equal to the number in the dividend minus the number in the divisor.

This follows from the corresponding rule in multiplication, since the divisor times the quotient equals the dividend. The following may make this clear:

Multiplication: $\underset{\text{2 decimals}}{33.33} \times \underset{\text{1 decimal}}{0.3} = \underset{\text{3 decimals}}{9.999}$

Division: $\dfrac{9.999 \text{ (3 decimals)}}{0.3 \text{ (1 decimal)}} = 33.33 \text{ (2 decimals)}$

EXAMPLE 5-5

$$\frac{XX.X}{X.X}$$

The quotient field should be three digits long and will have no decimal places. Alternatively,

$$\frac{XX.X}{X.X} = \frac{XX.X}{X.X} \times \frac{10}{10} = \frac{XXX}{XX}$$

giving the same result.

EXAMPLE 5-6

$$\frac{XX.XXX}{X.XX}$$

The quotient field should be five digits long and will have one decimal place. Alternatively,

$$\frac{XX.XXX}{X.XX} = \frac{XX.XXX}{X.XX} \times \frac{100}{100} = \frac{XXXX.X}{XXX}$$

EXAMPLE 5-7

$$\frac{XX.XXX}{.XX}$$

It is required that the answer be rounded to two decimal places. The dividend must have two zeros added to the right-hand end by shifting, giving XX.XXX00. (In some computers this can most conveniently be accomplished by multiplying by 100.) The quotient field will then be seven digits long with three decimal places. The third place will be eliminated by rounding, leaving the desired two-place accuracy.

EXAMPLE 5-8

$$\frac{XXX}{.X}$$

Application of the rule in this case would result in a negative number of decimal places, which is meaningless. To solve this case the dividend must first have one decimal place added at the right, giving XXX.0. The quotient field will then be four digits long with no decimal places. Alternatively,

$$\frac{XXX}{.X} = \frac{XXX}{.X} \times \frac{10}{10} = \frac{XXX0}{X}$$

Remainder

In the examples given so far we have not considered the remainder. Divide instructions normally provide for a remainder to be calculated and stored in a special area, usually adjacent to the quotient.

EXAMPLE 5-9

$$\frac{99.99}{4.4}$$

This will be calculated by the computer in integers as

$$\frac{9999}{44}$$

which is equal to 0227 with a remainder of 11. We must ascertain separately the position of the decimal points, obtaining the answer 022.7 with a remainder of .11. Thus

$$\frac{99.99}{4.4} = 022.7 + \frac{.11}{4.4} \qquad \text{or} \qquad 22.7 + 0.025$$

This answer for the quotient, i.e., 22.7, cannot be assumed to be accurate to one decimal place. If the remainder had been 0.22 or greater, it would have been necessary to round up the last digit (0.7) to 0.8.

To overcome this difficulty where one decimal place accuracy is required, the calculation should be modified to give a quotient with two decimal places. This is then half-adjusted in the usual way. The answer will then be accurate to one decimal place regardless of the value of the remainder, which can, therefore, be ignored.

Thus we would program to calculate

$$\frac{99.990}{4.4}$$

obtaining a quotient of 022.72, which would then be rounded to one decimal place.

Using this technique, *we are not usually interested in the value of the remainder.* (The only likely exception is where we might require to know, for some special reason, if the division works out exactly with no remainder.) The general procedure, then, is to program to obtain the quotient with one more decimal place than required in the final answer and then eliminate this last decimal place by rounding.

Rule

Before a division is attempted, a test must be made to see if the divisor is zero.

Division by zero cannot be performed by any means. Suitable alternative action must be allowed for in the program. The zero divisor may be a valid possibility, in which case a suitable message or routine should be provided. If the zero divisor is *not* a valid possibility, an error message will be required.

Note: The normal algebraic rules of division apply:

1. Dividends may be zero in which case the quotient will be zero. This is a valid division and requires no special testing.
2. The sign of the quotient is determined by the rule that similar signs in dividend and divisor give a positive quotient while opposite signs give a negative quotient.

PROBLEM 5-1 (mandatory)

Monthly Stock Turnover

OBJECTIVE

To calculate the number of times each inventory stock item has "turned over" during the month.

SOURCE DATA

Punched cards:

INVENTORY MASTER (01)	Col.	*RECEIPTS (02)*	Col.	*ISSUES (03)*	Col.
Card Code (01)	1-2	Card Code (02)	1-2	Card Code (03)	1-2
Stock No.	5-8	Stock No.	5-8	Stock No.	5-8
Description	9-28				
Balance	29-36	Amount	29-36	Amount	29-36
Month	79-80	Month	79-80	Month	79-80

PROCEDURE

1. Update inventory master balance with receipts and issues and punch a new master card with the month updated.
2. Sequence check on the stock number. There must be *one* master card for each stock item.
3. For each stock item,

$$\text{Average balance} = \frac{\text{old balance + new balance}}{2}$$

$$\text{e.g.,} \quad \frac{\$8000.00 + 4000.00}{2} = \$6000.00$$

$$\text{Turnover} = \frac{\text{issues}}{\text{average balance}} \qquad \text{e.g.,} \quad \frac{\$10{,}000.00}{\$6000.00} = 1.67$$

OUTPUT

Report of the following format:

STOCK NO.	*DESCRIPTION*	*OLD BALANCE*	*RECEIPTS*	*ISSUES*	*NEW BALANCE*	*TURN-OVER*
1212	Plywood 1/4	$ 8,000.00	$ 6,000.00	$10,000.00	$ 4,000.00	1.67
1213	Plywood 3/8	40,000.00	0.00	40,000.00	0.00	2.00
1214	Plywood 1/2	15,000.00	5,000.00	15,000.00	5,000.00	1.50
1216	Plywood 3/4	10,000.00	10,000.00	8,000.00	12,000.00	0.73
Totals		$ _______	$ _______	$ _______	$ _______	

Note well: Always check for zero divisor prior to dividing.
Flowchart, code, test, and fully document this problem.

PROBLEM 5-2 (mandatory)

Assume the following constants are stored in your computer's memory in decimal format:

NAME	*VALUE*
X	50.35
Y	88.888
Z	0.21

Give the coding for the following calculations:

1. Divide Y by 4 and round to one decimal place.
2. Divide Y by Z and round to two decimal places.
3. Calculate (Y X Z)/X and round to three decimal places.

PROBLEM 5-3

Inventory Unit Costs

OBJECTIVE

To calculate the unit cost of each inventory item.

SOURCE DATA

Inventory cards:

	COLUMNS
Card code (01)	1-2
Location	3-4
Stock number	5-8
Description	9-28
Total cost (XXXXXX.XX)	29-36
Quantity (number of items on hand)	37-41
Month	79-80

PROCEDURE

1. There is one card only per stock number.
2. For each stock number, calculate and print

$$\text{Unit cost} = \frac{\text{Total cost}}{\text{Quantity}} \qquad \text{(three decimals)}$$

3. Provide and test for zero and negative values.
4. Provide for totals by location and for final totals of cost.

6

Program Writing and Testing

PROGRAM WRITING

In this section we shall consider flowcharting, coding, and desk-checking practices. While there are no universally accepted standards, the programmer may find the following suggestions useful. (See also Chapter 8 on documentation and standardization.)

Flowcharting

The first step in program analysis is to obtain a clear understanding of the overall problem and in particular the format of the input and output. In the case of the input, especially, there will not only be the format of each input record to consider but also the number of different kinds of record and the sequence in which they occur. The output may involve detail printing, several levels of totals, error messages, and so on. If necessary, draw examples of typical sets of input and output records, considering all possibilities including the possibility of errors in input data. Only when all this is clearly in mind can flowcharting begin.

The overall basic logic of the program must now be visualized clearly. If the program is a complicated one, it may be preferable to start off with a "block diagram" or "main line logic" flowchart. In this the fine detail is omitted and each geometric figure or block may represent several related steps. The block diagram should not occupy more than one or two pages. See Figure 6-1 for an example.

When this is clearly established, detailed flowcharting can begin. The following rules should be observed.

1. Each page should be numbered and identified with the job name and number, and programmer name and date.

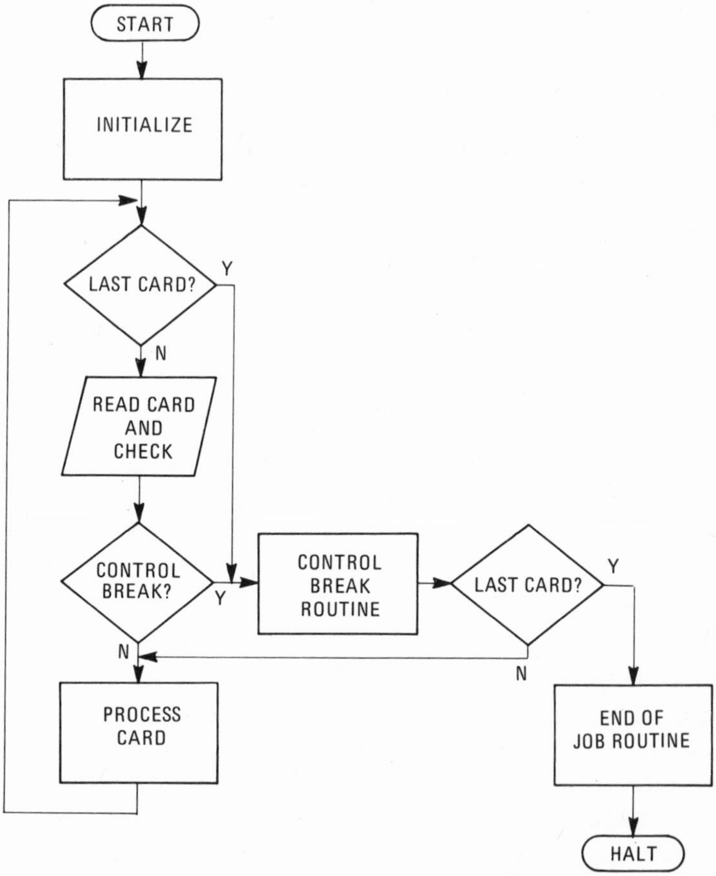

Fig. 6-1. Block Diagram of Simple Control Break.

2. Processing should, where possible, travel from left to right and top to bottom. It is permissible to disregard this rule if it results in a clearer and neater flowchart by avoiding the use of too many connectors on one page. In this case it is *essential* that the flowlines be marked with arrows to show the direction of flow. It is better, in fact, if *all* flowlines are so marked.
3. The description in the blocks should be in plain English except that *unambiguous* abbreviations may be used. If possible, use the same names for fields as are used in the program coding.
4. Cross reference the flowchart to the coding by inserting the major instruction labels in or adjacent to the block, as shown in Figure 3-7. This will greatly assist debugging and maintenance or modification of the program.
5. In general, flowchart first the flowpath that will occur most frequently, leaving the branches to other routines incomplete. Then go back to the next most frequent flowpath and complete it and so on, concluding with error routines. When finished, check carefully that there are no loose ends. All flowpaths must continue until they end in a terminal symbol (STOP).
6. Do not show every little detail, especially if it is a standard routine, such as half-adjusting. A good cross referencing to the coding will enable an interested reader to check these items easily and quickly.
7. All flowcharts should be in pencil to facilitate change during development. *The programmer's most useful asset is the eraser.*
8. The flowchart should avoid the technical terms of the particular language being coded. It should, indeed, be language-independent so that the flowchart will still serve in the event of translating the program to another language and also so that a person not familiar with the language can read it.
9. The next step is to design the print layout and if necessary the card, tape, or disk record layouts.

Coding

Under no circumstances should coding be started until the flowchart is complete. (It may not be in its final form, of course, but all logic paths must have been thoroughly analyzed.)

The coding *must* follow the flowchart. In the first place, the flowchart is presumably correct in its logic. In the second place, there is nothing more confusing to another programmer than trying to follow coding that does not agree with the flowchart.

Even though the coding follows the flowchart, there is still room for minor variation in the detail, since the flowchart does not show all the detail. Follow the same rule as in flowcharting, completing the main flowline first and then going to the next most important flowline. In any case, watch for unnecessary jumping about and duplication of instructions.

Use literals or "immediate" instructions if available and where convenient. They make the program easier to follow.

Do not use long error messages. They waste memory space.

Keep a separate coding sheet on hand for declaratives.

Instruction Labels. Use a simple, logical system. In a small program, variety in the type of label names may not be confusing, but in a large one it can be. For instance, if in a 40-page program there are instructions BRANCH TO JOE, BRANCH TO NEXT, etc., it can be challenging to find just where these instructions are. It also becomes brain-teasing to think up new labels after the first dozen or so.

A simple system is to assign a letter to each major section of the coding, starting with A for the first and following in sequence. Within each section, labels are assigned in sequence, as required, starting with A10, then A20, etc. The next section will have labels B10, B20, etc. It will be seen that there can be no duplication of labels, nine additional labels can be inserted if required without spoiling the sequence, no brainwracking is required to think of new labels, and, most important, any label can easily be found because of the logical sequence (see Example 3-1).

Do not use the letters I or O as these may be misread by the keypunch operator as one or zero.

At the beginning of each major segment should be a major comment block describing the routine. In addition, meaningful comments should be inserted throughout the routine.

In a very large program with many sections, a label in a given section *which is referred to in an instruction outside that section* may have a descriptive suffix added. This will help to make the outside instruction more meaningful. For instance, the label A10 in the card-reading section of the program may be referred to by an instruction in the section F as follows:

```
F10   ____
      ____
      ____
      B      A10
```

If the suffix READ is added to the label making it A10READ, then the instruction

```
B     A10READ
```

is a branch to the A section which clearly deals with card reading.

This technique is necessary only in large programs and in a label referred to from outside its own section.

Declarative Labels. These labels should *not* follow a system similar to instruction labels but should be as self-explanatory as possible.

Prefixes or suffixes like -IN, -OT should be standardized for all labels having some feature in common. For example, CARDIN could be the card input area, ACCTIN the account number in the input area, etc. AMTOT could be the field reserved for AMOUNT in the output area, etc.

A label whose meaning is not immediately obvious should be explained in the comments section of the coding sheet.

See Appendix B for an example of a fully documented program depicting these standards.

All coding should be in pencil. Remember, *the programmer's most useful asset is the eraser.*

Desk Checking

Much machine time can be saved by adequate desk checking. This can vary from a cursory look over the coding sheets to a detailed, manually calculated, follow-through of many input records to see what happens to them in the program as written.

Desk checking is best done using the printout of the punched source program rather than the original coding sheets so as to catch punching errors. Basic checking would include

1. Checks to see that all labels referenced in the operand column have been defined only once in the label column.
2. References to fields are to the correct end, i.e., left or right as appropriate.
3. Required length specifiers or other field length defining devices are included.
4. Unconditional branch or STOP to prevent instructions from running into declaratives.
5. Branches are made to valid addresses.
6. Correct conditional branches are made after a COMPARE operation.
7. The END or DEND card is included.

Remember the rule: *No program can be expected to work the first time.* You can always find one more error by more checking.

Card Decks. Write on the first card:

F/C, your name and the program name or number.

Write on the back of the last card:

L/C.

Write on the top edge:

program name or number and your initials.

Never throw away an old object deck until the new one has been thoroughly tested.

Never throw away the source deck.

If you correct errors in the object deck by "patching," *remember to correct the corresponding errors in the source deck before reassembling. This is very easy to overlook.*

Translating the Source Program

The procedure here will depend on the particular computer and facilities supplied by the manufacturer. Appendix C gives further information.

It should be noted that a successful translation free of diagnostic errors does not necessarily mean that the program will work correctly or will even work at all. This can only be verified by thorough testing of the object program.

TESTING AND DEBUGGING

Your program will not work the first time you try it. Therefore, you must be prepared to use a logical approach to finding out what is wrong. Much time can be wasted by random checking of the program with no plan of attack in mind. On the other hand, most bugs in a program are relatively easy to find if the problem is approached intelligently.

There are three major types of error that may occur. The program may not assemble properly, it may assemble satisfactorily but not execute properly, or it may assemble and run properly but give wrong answers.

Incorrect Assembly

The ease with which errors are found here depends largely on the quality of the diagnostic messages provided by the writer of the compiler. The only general point to note is that often errors are indicated in one instruction when the real trouble is in another instruction, e.g., a declarative label mis-spelled. Details to watch for here are confusion between the number 1 and the letter I, and the letter O and number 0.

Hang-up on Execution

This is probably the commonest type of problem. The first thing to do is to find out at what instruction the program has hung up. *This is vital.* In addition any indicator lights or diagnostic messages should be noted. It is also most desirable to obtain a memory dump. This is a printout of the entire contents of memory at the time of the hang-up. If it is later found to be necessary for debugging but has not been taken, the entire test may have to be repeated.

Having found at which instruction the program stopped, refer to the object program listing to see what the instruction is and what its operands are.

Check that the instruction is valid and appropriate.

Check the value of each operand field in the memory dump to see that its value is what you suppose it to be and that it has all necessary delimiters, signs, etc.

If the operands appear to be correct, check the instruction itself *in the memory dump.* It may have been changed or destroyed accidentally.

If the operand fields do not have the values you expected, examine the values they do have and see if you can get a clue from these. One possibility that should not be overlooked is incorrect punching of the input data.

If the memory dump shows that the instruction or operand fields have been completely destroyed, the trouble is probably in some other instruction that has been executed earlier. Lack of adequate field definition in a MOVE instruction is a very common cause here. An examination of adjacent instructions or operand fields to see which other ones have been destroyed may give a clue.

Another common cause of this type of error is improper definition of input or output areas.

If all efforts to locate the trouble fail, try rerunning the program with the addition of frequent, suitably placed printouts of selected portions of memory. This may give a clue as to *when* an instruction is destroyed, for instance.

Incorrect Answers

This is often the most difficult problem to solve. Frequently the cause is incorrect logic in the program, which indicates an error in the analysis of the problem and in the flowchart. For example, a common student error in Problem 3-2 is to compare the customer's new balance to the *next* customer's limit. Obviously, therefore, the first step is to look over the flowchart critically for errors of this kind. Where the detail is not spelled out in the flowchart, the coding itself will have to be studied.

When this analysis fails to give the solution, a useful technique is to rerun the test, simplifying the input and reducing it to the absolute minimum necessary to operate the program. For instance, in a simple control break problem, reduce the number of cards in each group to two and make the numbers to be manipulated simple.

It is necessary to verify which cards have been processed, especially if some are processed satisfactorily but the program hangs up on later ones. Also check carefully that the data cards are correct.

Usually the only approach in these types of problem is to mentally process the actual test cards through the program, comparing the results you calculate with what the problem specifies you should have obtained and what the computer actually produced.

In some cases, where the computer produces a completely unexpected output, such as an error message, where no error in the input data exists, following the program *backwards* from the error message to the conditional branch instruction that sent the computer to that routine may help. Inspection of the memory dump of the operand fields of this COMPARE instruction may give the necessary clue.

Obviously, program debugging is made easier with practice and experience. In all cases random checking of all possible errors will only waste time. The approach to follow is

1. Observe the readily available facts.
2. Use these facts to eliminate some of the possible causes, leaving others as the likely troublemaker.

3. Look for more evidence to further eliminate some of these possible causes. Maybe further testing will be necessary.
4. Continue narrowing down the possible causes in this way until the answer becomes obvious.

Finally, assume nothing and suspect everything.

Final Testing

All the immediately apparent errors having been eliminated, it is still necessary to perform comprehensive final testing with realistic input data. If successful, these results, input, and output, should be filed as part of the documentation of the job.

Realistic input data may be actual "live" data being used in the installation in the existing procedures or they may be specially prepared. In any case, it is important to observe a few precautions.

In at least one test card, all fields should have digits other than zero in all columns, and values should be chosen such that all answer fields should contain no zeros. It is quite easy to write a program that works correctly for an amount of $127.00 but not for $127.98.

Tests for negative conditions in all fields should be provided.

As far as is reasonably practical, every flowpath should be tested. In extremely complicated programs this may not be practical because of the large number of possible paths. However, even in this case, as many conditions as possible must still be checked out.

The results must be very carefully checked. If any error is found, debugging must be resumed, of course, and when it is complete, *all final testing must be repeated* to guard against the danger that the correcting of one error has introduced others.

Finally, programs, especially larger ones, should be processed using "live" data. If possible, an entire file should be rerun and checked against previously obtained results.

PROBLEMS

PROBLEM 6-1

What is the advantage, if any, in a large program of first drawing an overall summary flowchart?

PROBLEM 6-2

For what two reasons should the descriptions in a flowchart be written in plain non-technical terms?

PROBLEM 6-3

Some programmers draw the flowchart after coding the instructions. Why is this a bad practice?

PROBLEM 6-4

Why should test data include the largest possible values in the fields, as well as negative reversing entries for all amounts?

PROBLEM 6-5

Some computers such as the IBM 360 can produce automatic core dumps if the program hangs up on an execute error. What is the advantage of this feature?

PROBLEM 6-6

A program is initially written or partially rewritten. It is assembled, tested, and submitted to the computer operations department. It is run twice a month and works well. At the end of six months, however, it hangs up on an execute error. There is nothing wrong with the computer. Suggest possible reasons for the hang-up. Where should the investigation start?

7

Tables and Table Look-up

Tables are frequently used in business calculations. Common examples are the income tax table for computing tax based on salary, the unemployment insurance table for computing deductions, rate tables for customer's utility billing, and interest tables.

It will be necessary, therefore, in programming, to have some efficient means by which the computer can use the appropriate tables. The method of determining an employee's income tax deduction that was probably used in solving Problem 2-2 (i.e., repeated conditional branching) is very inefficient when the number of entries in the table is more than about five or six. Because many tables have dozens or even hundreds of entries, this method becomes completely impractical. Fortunately, we can make use of the stored program's unique ability to modify its own instructions to solve this problem.

TERMINOLOGY

The entries in a table have technical names as follows:

Argument: the reference data or field used to specify a particular entry, e.g., the taxable income in an income tax table.

There are usually two arguments to be considered. The *search argument* is the argument whose value is given by the input data. It is the employee's actual taxable income in the income tax example. The *table argument* is one of the values in the table, usually the one we are currently examining to see if it matches the search argument.

The *function* is the value we read from the table corresponding to the particular table argument. It is the piece of information we hope to acquire from the table, such as the tax rate. Each argument in a table can have only one corresponding function value, but a particular function value may correspond to a unique argument or to a range of arguments.

TYPES OF TABLES

There are two main types of tables.

Discrete Tables

These tables have a unique value of the table argument for each entry.

Consider, for example, a payroll problem. Employees work on an hourly basis. Their pay is based on the job on which they work. Job numbers are assigned to each job, and the employee is paid at the rate for the job. For job 1 his rate may be \$3.25 per hour, for job 2 it may be \$4.15, etc.

If the employee worked for 10 hours on job 2, he would submit a time card containing, among other required information, his employee number, job 2, and 10 hours. Neither the rate of pay nor the extended hours times rate (wage) need be entered on his time card. These will be calculated by the computer program.

The program contains a table of job numbers with the corresponding rate of pay for each job, as shown in Figure 7-1. The information on the time card is keypunched, and the card is read into the computer. The program must find job 2 in the table and locate the rate of pay, $4.15. It will then calculate earnings by multiplying the 10 hours punched on the card by the rate of $4.15.

Job Numbers and Rate of Pay Table

JOB NUMBER (ARGUMENT)	*RATE OF PAY (FUNCTION) ($)*
01	3.25
02	4.15
04	4.65
05	3.75
.	.
.	.
.	.

Fig. 7-1.

In this example, the search argument is the employee's job 2. The table argument is the job number in the table. The function, the information that is required, is the rate of pay.

Segmented Tables

In this type of table, each argument is specified as a range of values.

Consider, for example, the income tax problem given in Problem 2-2. The table is provided in Figure 7-2, with the addition of a rate for taxable income over $10,000.

TAXABLE INCOME (ARGUMENT) ($)	*TAX (FUNCTION) ($)*
0-2000	10% of taxable income
2001-4000	200 + 15% of income over 2000
4001-6000	500 + 20% of income over 4000
6001-8000	900 + 22% of income over 6000
8001-10,000	1340 + 25% of income over 8000
10,001 and over	1840 + 30% of income over 10,000

Fig. 7-2. Income Tax Table

The table argument is the taxable income. In this example, the function is composed of two parts: the rate of tax (e.g., 15%) and a correction adjustment for that rate (e.g., $200).

SEQUENTIAL AND NONSEQUENTIAL TABLES

Normally, all tables will be sequential; i.e., the first entry will contain the lowest value of the argument, the second will contain the next lowest, and so on, with the final entry containing the highest value. This is the case in both the examples given.

Although it is not absolutely essential for programming purposes that arguments be sequential, it facilitates programming to such an extent that nonsequential tables will not be considered in this text.

STORING THE TABLE IN THE COMPUTER

Before the program can make use of the table, it must be stored in the computer memory. This is commonly accomplished by one of two methods. By the first method, it may be stored in memory when the program is loaded, as part of the declarative section of the program.

By the second method, it may be stored after the program is loaded. The table may be read in as data, with, for example, one table argument and function per card. The program will expect these to be the first cards read. It will ensure that the arguments are in ascending sequence and will store them consecutively in an area in memory allocated for the table.

Problem 7-1 may be written with the table assigned by declaratives as in the first method. Problem 7-2 specifies that the second method of storing a table be used.

In either case, the entries in a table are usually stored in consecutive order, with argument 1 followed by function 1, then argument 2 followed by function 2, and so on. As a rule, all table arguments are defined with the same length, and all functions are also defined with the same length. Figure 7-3A illustrates this schematically for the job number and rate of pay table.

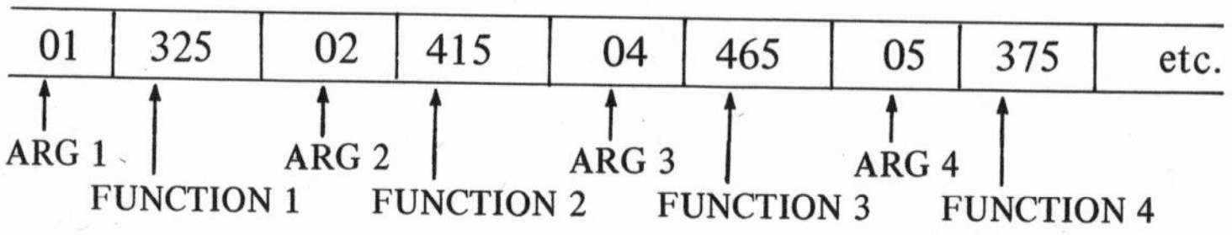

Fig. 7-3A.

Alternatively, in high-level languages such as Fortran, Cobol, and PL/I, the argument and the function are often stored in separate tables, as depicted in Figure 7-3B.

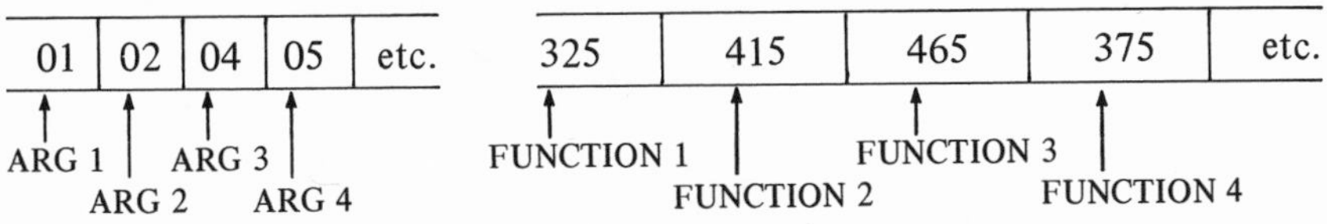

Fig. 7-3B.

PROCEDURE FOR SEARCHING DISCRETE TABLES

Figure 7-4 illustrates the job number and rate of pay table. The address of the first argument in the table is given the label of the table, called here TAB. For this example, TAB refers to core location 2000. The address of the first function is RATE, at core location 2002.

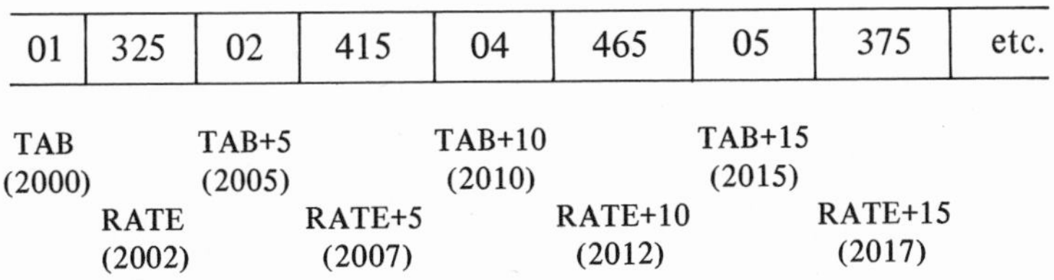

Fig. 7-4.

Assume a time card is read containing job 2, which is referred to by the label JOB. This search argument is compared to the first table argument, which is the contents of TAB at location 2000. Since 02 is higher than the table argument 01, the comparison is unequal. We now want to compare JOB to the next argument. Instead of writing a compare instruction for each test as was probably done in Problem 2-2, we can use the same compare instruction. We merely have to change the address of the second operand by increasing TAB to TAB+5 or core address 2000 to 2005. (Since the number of digits in the argument is two and in the function three, there are five positions between arguments.)

We repeat the test by comparing JOB to the second entry in the table. This will give an equal comparison. Having located the required rate of pay, at RATE+5 or location 2005, the program branches out of the routine to subsequent calculation of earnings.

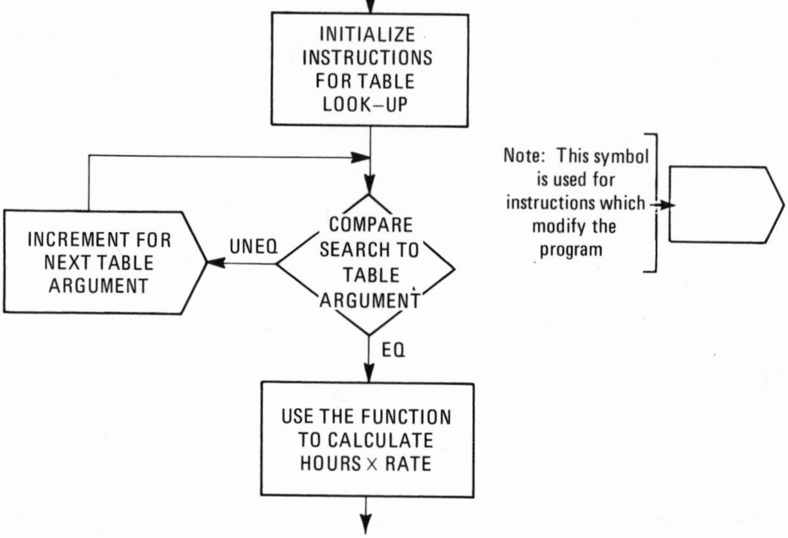

Fig. 7-5. Discrete Table Search (No Provision for Missing Entries).

The flowchart is shown in Figure 7-5 and the PLC coding follows. How table look-up routines are actually coded will depend on the particular language and computer being used. See Appendix A for examples.

The PLC coding shows first the defining of the table. The first argument, job 01, is stored in the 2-position field labeled TAB. The first function, \$3.25, is stored in the 3-position field labeled RATE. The remaining entries do not have to be labeled.

Initialization by the RESET command will be clearer after going through the example coding, using the same search argument, job 2, as before. We compare the contents of JOB to the contents of TAB. Since the comparison is unequal, we add 5 to the second operand of TEST so that the next time we will compare JOB to TAB+5. Similarly we add 5 to the second operand of CALC so that the instruction is modified to multiply HRS by RATE+5. The program branches back to TEST, where JOB is now compared to TAB+5.

PLC Coding of Figure 7-5

LABEL	*OPERATION*	*OPERANDS*	*COMMENTS*
TAB	DEFINE	2, CONTAINS '01'	Define the table
RATE	DEFINE	3, CONTAINS '325'	
	DEFINE	2, CONTAINS '02'	
	DEFINE	3, CONTAINS '415'	
	DEFINE	2, CONTAINS '04'	
	DEFINE	3, CONTAINS '465'	
	. . .		
START	RESET	OPERAND 2 OF TEST TO 'TAB'	Initialize addresses
	RESET	OPERAND 2 OF CALC TO 'RATE'	
TEST	COMPARE	JOB TO TAB	
	BE	CALC	
	ADD	'5' TO OPERAND 2 OF TEST	Modify addresses
	ADD	'5' TO OPERAND 2 OF CALC	
	B	TO TEST	
CALC	MULT	HRS BY RATE	Subsequent processing

Since the result is equal, the program branches to CALC, where HRS from the card is multiplied by the contents of RATE+5.

It can now be seen that the modified operands must be initialized at the start of the routine to their original addresses. Otherwise, the search on the next card read would begin with the operands still containing the addresses as modified by the table look-up for the preceding card.

MISSING ENTRIES

It is quite possible that not all possible job numbers in the range 00-99 actually exist in the table. A particular job number may never have been assigned or may have become obsolete and been removed. What will happen with our program if, for instance, job 3 does not exist in the table, but a data card with this job number is read? The naive programmer might assume that since this *should* not occur, it *will* not. However, one of the cardinal rules in programming is that if something possibly *can* happen, then it *will*. There might be a keypunching error or an error on the original time ticket, or there could actually be a new job 3 of which the data-processing department has not yet been advised. Indeed, this last possibility occurs very frequently. Let us see, then, what happens with flowchart Figure 7-5 in this situation and the coding example given previously.

Comparing the search argument job 3 with the table argument 01, we find it is unequal, in fact high. The same is true of table argument 02. Next we compare it to 04. It is again unequal, but note that this time it is *low*. If the program is allowed to continue running, it would compare with succeeding job numbers 05, 06, 07, 08, etc., all the way to the last entry. Indeed, if the process is not stopped, it will continue through memory past the end of the table. Obviously, this is a serious programming error. What we should have programmed for was the possibility that the entry search argument was not in the table at all.

The problem can be solved quite easily by testing not merely for unequal but for high and low. If the search argument is higher than the table argument, the search can continue, but if it is ever lower, then we know that it is not in the table. Figure 7-6 shows the corrected flowchart.

Suppose now that the highest job number in the table is 50 and that an input card with a job number of 60 is read in. The table will be searched, each test giving a high comparison, including the comparison with the last table argument—50. The search will then continue past the end of the table, giving a programming error. This problem can be overcome by the addition of a dummy entry at the end of the table with the largest possible job number argument, i.e., 99 in this case. The last comparison will then always give a low result, which indicates an error condition. If we assume that there is no valid job 99, the only case where this procedure will fail is if the erroneous search argument is 99. This can be checked by a simple

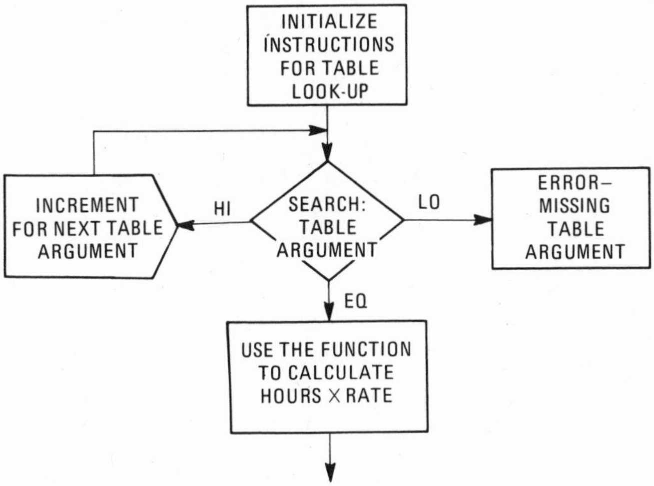

Fig. 7-6. Discrete Table Search (Detection of Missing Entries).

test to eliminate this possible error before starting the search routine. The last argument entry in a table, then, should always be a field of 9's.

PROCEDURE FOR SEARCHING SEGMENTED TABLES

The programming for a problem involving a table based on segments such as the income tax table is very similar to that for the discrete table. First, however, we must consider the format in which the table is stored, since the argument as given in Problem 2-2 contains two values–an upper and a lower limit. It is only necessary to store one of these in the table. It should be apparent with a little thought that we need store only the upper limit. Then, if the search argument is higher than the table argument, the search is to be continued exactly as in the case of discrete tables.

However, the flowchart as used for discrete tables will not work without modification, because it is most unlikely that the search argument is going to be exactly equal to an upper limit. What we are trying to test here is if the search argument is *between* the lower and upper limits.

02000	0000	10	04000	0200	15	06000	0500	20	etc.

Fig. 7-7.

Figure 7-7 shows the income tax table as it may be stored in memory. The first argument, $2000, is followed by the first correction adjustment, $0000, and the rate, 10%. The rest of the table follows sequentially.

Consider an amount of taxable income of $5000. This search argument is compared to the first entry in the table and is higher. It is necessary, then, just as in the preceding example, to compare to the next table argument. This result will also be higher. We then compare to the next argument. Since the result is low and the preceding one was high, we have found the range of taxable incomes that contains the required rate and adjustment.

What if the entry argument were exactly $6000? The correct rate would be the same one as for $5000. In other words, we have reached the correct segment of the table if the entry argument is *less than or equal to* the table argument. The flowchart is then as shown in Figure 7-8.

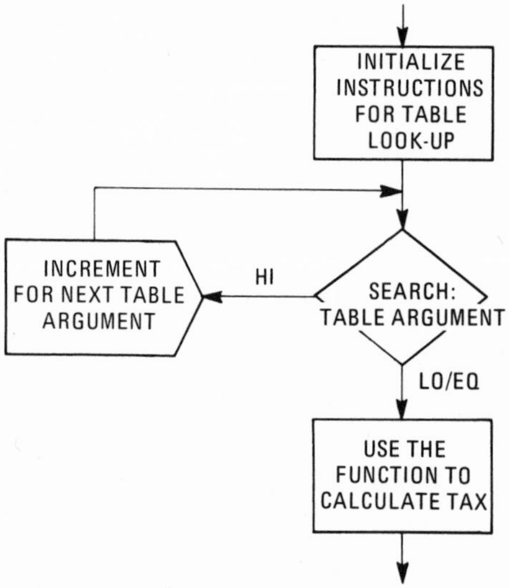

Fig. 7-8. Segmented Table Search.

Once again, as in the previous example, the last argument in the table should contain the highest possible value–in this case $99,999–for taxable incomes exceeding $10,000.

In this particular example, there will be no errors initiated by missing table arguments as in Figure 7-6, since any possible taxable income defined in a five-digit field must be equal to or less than at least one of the table arguments.

Note: The precise coding technique for defining tables and programming table search will vary considerably according to the particular computer language being used. Appendix A gives several examples.

PROBLEMS

PROBLEM 7-1 (mandatory)

Table Look-up–Income Tax Deduction

INPUT

Card format as shown:

	COLUMNS
Card code (22)	1-2
Store, department, employee number	3-4, 5-7, 8-11
Name	13-33
Month	34-35
Gross pay (XXXX.XX)	51-56
Exemption (XXX.XX)	61-65

PROCEDURE

1. Cards are supposed to be in sequence by employee number within department within store, one card per employee.
2. Calculate the monthly tax deduction for each employee based on his taxable income (gross pay less tax exemption). Tax deduction = rate X taxable income.
3. Provide total gross pay and tax deduction for employee, department, store, and final totals.

OUTPUT

A report providing all relevant information about the employee as well as required totals.

TAXABLE INCOME ($)	*RATE (%)*
Up to 100.00	0.0
100.01-150.00	4.0
150.01-220.00	8.0
220.01-350.00	10.0
350.01-500.00	14.0
500.01-650.00	16.5
650.01-800.00	18.0
800.01 and over	20.0

REQUIRED

Working program with full documentation.

PROBLEM 7-2 (mandatory)

Table Look-up

OBJECTIVE

To extend employee payroll time cards (hours X rate). When an employee works on a job, the job number and the hours worked (but not the rate) are entered on a time slip and keypunched onto cards. At the end of the week, these time cards are sorted by employee number and then processed on the computer to calculate wages. Job numbers and the rate of pay for each job are stored by the program. The rate for each time card is found by searching through the job number table.

INPUT

	JOB RATE TABLE CARD	*EMPLOYEE TIME CARD*
Card code	(21) 1-2	(22) 1-2
Job number	3-5	38-40
Rate (X.XXX)	6-9	–
Dept. number	–	5
Employee number	–	8-11
Name	–	13-32
Hours (XX.X)	–	41-43
Month	–	79-80

PROCEDURE

1. Read all the job rate table cards (21) in sequence of job number and store the job number and rate in a table. Job numbers may be any number from 000 to 999. Provide a table to accommodate about 100 different jobs, the last one being job 999.
2. Read the employee time cards (22) in employee number sequence. Using the job number on the card, find the rate for that job number from the table. Extend the employee's hours X rate.

If a time card contains a job number that is not in the table, output an error message.

OUTPUT

1. A report containing the following:

   Extended employee job cards, total hours and wage for each employee, and final total of hours and wage

Payroll – May 1971

DEPARTMENT	*EMPLOYEE NUMBER*		*JOB NUMBER*	*HOURS*	*RATE*	*WAGE*
9	1031	A J SMITH	319	40.0	4.505	180.20
				40.0 *		180.20 *
4	1037	J M JOHNSON	4	12.0	2.500	30.00

4	1037	J M JOHNSON	4	14.0	2.500	35.00
4	1037	J M JOHNSON	50	5.5	3.155	17.35
3	1037	J M JOHNSON	4	15.0	2.500	37.50
				46.5 *		119.85 *
		.				
		.				
		.				
FINAL TOTAL				418.5 **		1511.96 **

2. *Optional:* An additional report containing total hours and wages by department. Check the totals to the preceding report.

Department Wage Distribution – May 1971

DEPARTMENT	*HOURS*	*WAGE*
1	40.0	155.00
2	20.0	60.17
–	–	–
–	–	–
9	70.0	275.25
FINAL TOTAL	418.5 *	1511.96 *

PROBLEM 7-3 (exercise)

Conversion of Numeric Month to Alphabetic Month

Design a table and write a routine for the following:

1. The table will contain the 12 numeric months as arguments and the corresponding alphabetic months as functions; i.e., the first entry will be 01 JANUARY. The table is called MONTAB.
2. The input area contains the numeric month in a field called MONIN.
3. Using MONIN as the search argument, perform a TLU (table look-up) to locate the correct month in MONTAB. Transfer the alphabetic month from the table to a field called MONALF.

(This procedure can be used for printing the alphabetic month in the heading of a report.)

8

Standardization and Documentation

STANDARDIZATION

The purpose of standardization in programming is to ensure that all programs are similar in format to one another.

In the early days of programming the need for standards and documentation was not recognized. Programmers, even in a single organization, used their own individual techniques and personal preferences. This was not a serious problem in early small installations, especially as long as there were the same programmers constantly working on the same applications.

When the succeeding generation of larger and more complex computers came on the market, however, it was found necessary to translate all the old programs into the new languages and also to hire and train many more programmers for the ever-increasing volume and scope of work. Naturally, communications problems between the programmers in an installation became more difficult, and it became apparent that standardization of procedures would help to reduce the confusion.

Some suggestions for standardization have already been given in Chapter 6 in the section on program writing. The remainder of this chapter suggests standards for the documenting of each program.

DOCUMENTATION

Neither programs nor programmers are static. The latter change jobs from time to time, and the former frequently have to be reviewed and revised as conditions change. It follows that proper records of programs must be kept if confusion is to be avoided.

Documentation is a standardized approach to the organizing, preparing, maintaining, and filing of the program record. It acts as both a historical record and as a reference manual. It provides full reasons and details as to who developed the program, what it is about, and its current status.

Reasons for Documentation

For Programmers. It ensures that the programmer maintains a methodical approach to program writing.

It facilitates "team" programming so that a group of programmers may work on a single project.

It facilitates reviewing the program. If another programmer has to amend the program, he will be better able to understand the program and to identify the required change. Indeed, since the original programmer himself will no doubt quickly forget the program details, he will find the documentation necessary.

It facilitates translating into a new language.

For Others. It provides systems analysts with consistent comprehensive details of the programs. This will facilitate system revisions.

It provides the data-processing manager, consultants, auditors, and computer manufacturers' representatives with a useful view of the operations of the department. They will be better able to suggest improved controls and to assist in coordination and planning.

The preparation of these records need not be unduly time-consuming and laborious, since the bulk of the information will have been collected in the course of designing the program. What is required is a standardized format, so that the material is readily understood by any member of the programming organization.

While there is no universally accepted code of standards, there are some procedures which are extensively used, and we shall discuss these along with others which we have found useful. Each data-processing installation should establish those standards it considers desirable and the practising programmer should follow the procedures of the installation in which he is working. In this way, any other programmer in that installation can easily ascertain all the information he requires about any program, including even details as to why the program was written the way it was. In fact, the original programmer may well find this useful, since after a few months even his own program logic may appear obscure to him.

The Program File

The documentation should be maintained in a suitable file or folder. There are specially designed files now available which are well suited for this purpose.

The programs should be numbered. It does not matter whether the numbers are chronological (i.e., the first program written is 1, the second 2, etc.) or established by application (i.e., all general ledger programs have a certain prefix, all inventory programs another prefix, etc.).

If one individual is given the responsibility of assigning the numbers and recording them in a master list, there should be no duplication. The program number should appear on every document in the program file.

The file may be considered to consist of several sections as follows:

1. General section
   a. Title page. This includes program number and name, date, and name of programmer.
   b. Table of contents. Each page in the file should be numbered consecutively, including computer printouts.
   c. Purpose of program. One or two paragraphs stating concisely the

objectives of the program. If you find that this takes more than half a page, rewrite it.

d. Recipients of the report.

e. Frequency of the report (e.g., daily, weekly).

f. Controls. The control procedure set up to ensure accuracy should be specified.

g. The original authorization for the program. This will specify the person responsible in case of queries regarding the purpose of the program and for subsequent changes to the program.

2. Program details section. This section comprises the bulk of the file and includes the following:

a. Input and output formats. Cards, tape, disk, printer formats.

b. Flowcharts.

c. Current compiled listing. This must be dated so that it will be recognized as the most recent listing.

d. Description. Brief description of method of operation of the program with detailed description of special techniques, unusual instructions, assignment of switches and registers, restrictions, etc.

e. Sample test data. This will include listings of input data, output data, and a memory dump. It is also useful to retain test data in card form so that the original tests can easily be repeated after minor modifications have been made to the program.

f. Modifications. This will list the authorization, the programmer making the change, the date, and the nature of the change. It is also useful to include here the previous program listing showing how the changes were made. This is desirable in case the new compilation fails to work or in case the request for the change is canceled after the change has been made.

3. Operations section. This section is for the benefit of the operating department and may be duplicated in a special operator's manual. It should in any case be included as part of the main program documentation file. It will include the following:

a. Operating instructions. These will list such information as schedule of running job, estimate of time required, switch settings, special information about the input data organization and any control cards required, printer forms, printer control tapes, tape reels, disk packs, drives to use, etc.

b. Operator messages. All programmed messages to the operator should be described and the action to be taken on each message specified.

A fully documented program, written in IBM/360 Assembler language, is provided in Appendix B.

PROBLEMS

PROBLEM 8-1

Review the programs you have written in the light of the suggestions made in this chapter.

Revise the documentation of one of them to bring it to a professionally acceptable standard.

PROBLEM 8-2

You are the newly hired supervisor of programming. You discover that your firm has never adopted standards or conventions in its 5 years of computer operations. Each of the five programmers has adopted his own conventions, many of which are obscure to you. What arguments would you use to persuade your staff to adopt common standards?

PROBLEM 8-3

A programming department has many urgent top-priority programs to write and make operative. Is it desirable to postpone the documentation so that it may be done in a more leisurely manner at a later date?

9

Subroutines

A subroutine is a group of instructions written to perform a specific task, which is usually required to be executed at several different places in a large program. This could be done by repeating the instructions at each place, which would be very wasteful of memory. Alternatively, it could be done by branching to one set of instructions and using switches to enable the program to get back to the main program at the right place, which could become very complicated if the routine was to be used frequently.

Instead, most computers have special "linkage" instructions to enable the second method to be used without the necessity for setting and testing switches.

The advantages of using subroutines are:

1. A complex section may be written once and used by more than one part of the program. This practice saves space in the memory.
2. The subroutine may be used in other programs, even by other programmers.
3. By simplifying the structure of the program design, it permits better legibility and easier debugging.
4. It simplifies flowcharting.

EXAMPLE 9-1

The program may require that headings be printed at the top of each page. In the initializing part of the program, it is necessary to make sure that the headings start at the top of the page where the heading itself is printed. Then the program continues on to the main logic, such as reading the input, processing it, and printing detail. Eventually the program recognizes that sufficient printing has been done so that the bottom of the page has been reached. What is normally done is that the program will cause the printer forms to eject to start at the top of the next page. At this point we would like to be able to repeat what we did at the initial part of the program, that is, print headings once more. We do not want to rewrite all those instructions, but going back into the initial heading routine will lead us into the main logic part of the program again. Furthermore, there will be various places at which we want to print headings. We may recognize that we have reached the bottom of the page on printing an ordinary detail line or on a minor, intermediate, or major total. Hence, there are many points in the program at which we would like to print these headings.

It would be ideal if there were *one* heading routine that we could branch to, execute this heading routine, and then return to the main program. The process of doing this is one of setting up *subroutines* in the program. Each computer language can accommodate this situation normally by that language's own unique linkage, its own way of branching into the subroutine, and its own way of returning.

In general, what is required is an instruction that will branch to the subroutine and at the same time store somewhere the address of the next sequential instruction. This is the one that is to be carried out after the subroutine has been completed. At the end of the subroutine, a special branch instruction returns program control to this instruction, whose address has been specially retained.

The procedure is illustrated schematically in Figure 9-1.

FLOWCHARTING SUBROUTINES

An example of flowcharting for the program example of producing reports with multilevel control breaks as given in Chapter 4, Figure 4-7, is now provided in Figure 9-2. This is the same flowchart, providing for the following additions:

1. At each print operation, a count of the number of lines spaced is added to a line counter.

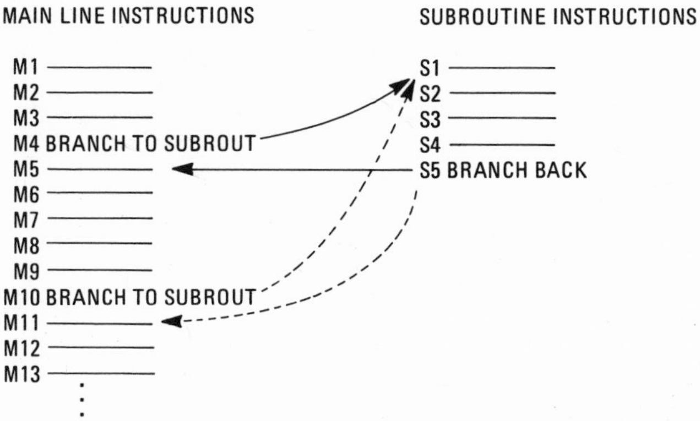

Fig. 9-1. Sequence of Instructions Followed is M1, M2, M3, M4, S1, S2, S3, S4, S5, M5, M6, M7, M8, M9, M10, S1, S2, S3, S4, S5, M11, M12, M13, etc.

2. At appropriate places in the program the line counter is checked for having exceeded the maximum permissible number of lines to be printed on a page.

If we have not exceeded that maximum number, we continue processing. Alternatively, if we have exceeded it, we branch through our program linkage to the page overflow subroutine. The page overflow subroutine is shown in Figure 9-3 as a separate flowchart from the main flowchart. The linkages are shown at the entry point where it has come from the main flowchart and at the bottom terminal point where it will return to the main flowchart.

This subroutine will execute the following:

1. Clear the line counter.
2. Skip to the top of the next page.
3. Print the required headings, including the page number.
4. Add to the page number counter.
5. Branch back to the next sequential instruction in the main program.

Note the following subroutine flowchart conventions:

1. The main line program. The subroutine is merely *referred* to by the main program. The subroutine symbol is a rectangle, *striped,* to identify (a) top left, the name or label of the subroutine; (b) top right, the page where it is located; and (c) bottom, its general description. The rectangle is treated as a complete process, the detail of which may be referred to by the reader if he wants. Note how much simpler the flowchart appears as contrasted to one in which all the details were included in with the main logic.

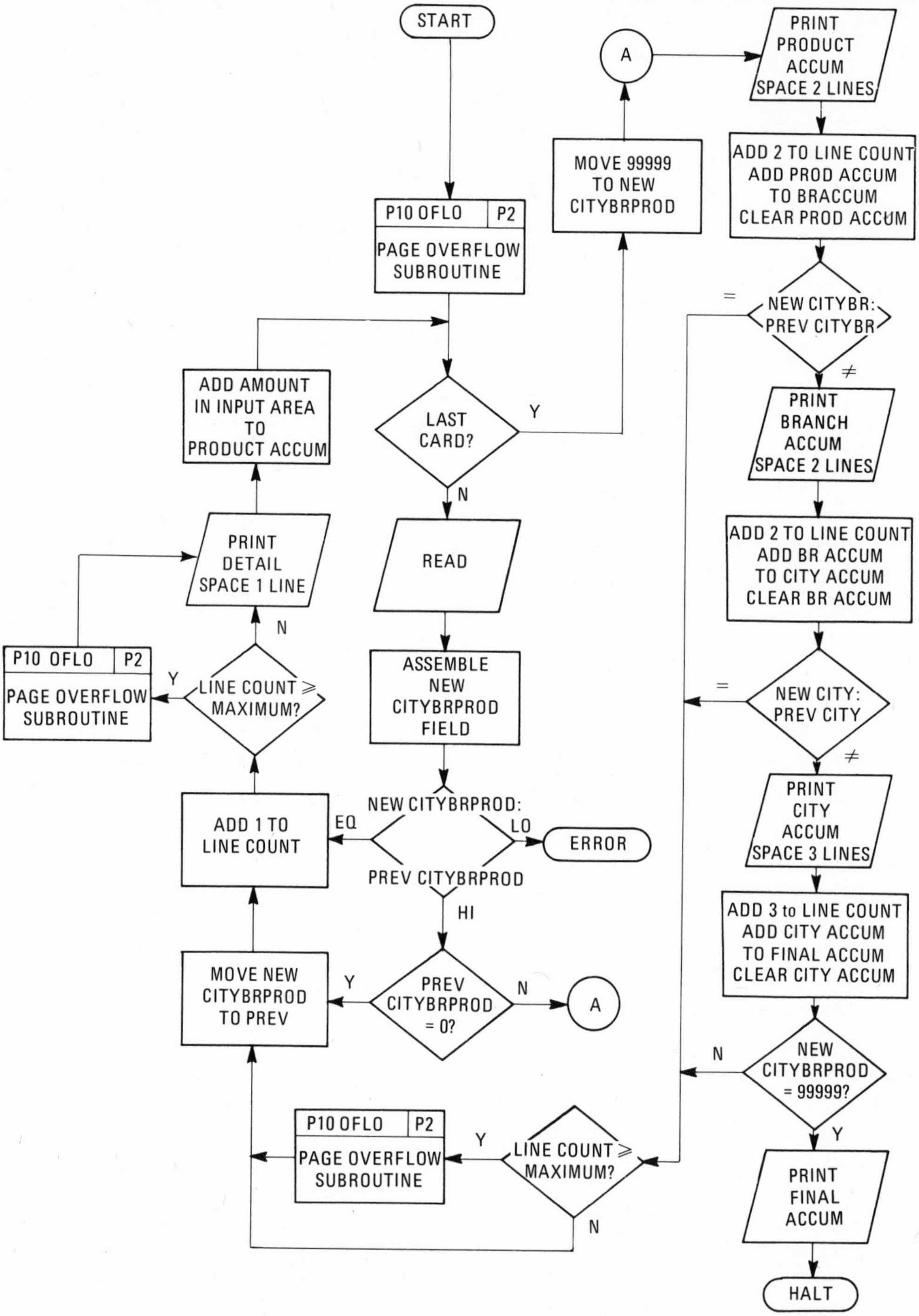

Fig. 9-2. Multilevel Control Break with Page Overflow.

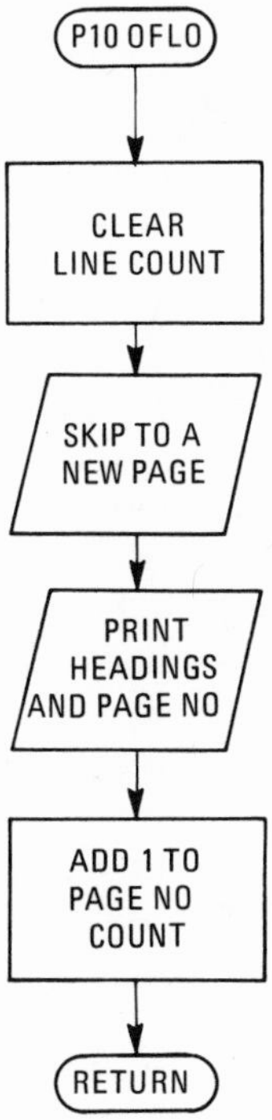

Fig. 9-3. Page Overflow Subroutine.

2. The subroutine.There is a heading to describe and identify the subroutine. The entry and exit points use the "terminal" symbol. Note that the subroutine is treated as a unique, separate program and therefore has its own terminal symbols. All other flowchart symbols are used normally.

These conventions should be strictly adhered to.

EXAMPLE 9-2

Table Look-up.

Frequently, table look-ups can be treated as subroutines. They do not have to be considered as part of the main line of the program where the main line is reading of input, sequence checking, testing for various card codes, etc., but not including any special, more complex operations. Table look-up would be a good example of a more complex operation that could be treated in many ways as a separate part of the program. All that is necessary before going into the table look-up subroutine is to have the search argument available to the table look-up subroutine. In this case, whether there is only one table look-up in the program or many, we can still write it as a subroutine. Where necessary, the program branches to the table look-up routine, locates the required table function, and returns to the main line of the program.

EXAMPLE 9-3

Multilevel Control Breaks

In Chapter 4 the problem of multilevel control breaks was described by means of the control word approach and also by means of the switching technique. In this example we will show how the problem can also be resolved by means of subroutines. Refer once more to Figure 4-7. In that example, we were performing control breaks according to (1) major, (2) intermediate, and, (3) minor. In this example, neither switches nor control words will be necessary. The general solution is similar to that used in the switching example to perform the control break according to, first, the major field, second, the intermediate field, and, third, the minor field. Each subroutine to accommodate the process required at each control break level need be written only once but will be referenced by the program from many points. The flowchart example following is self-explanatory (Figures 9-4 and 9-5).

MODULAR PROGRAMMING

As programs become larger in size and complexity, it becomes increasingly necessary to standardize and organize the programming approach. It becomes more essential to *segment* the program for purposes of clarity. One way to achieve this goal is to make use of modular programming. This approach consists of the following:

1. The main steps of the program, such as input, control break, and output, are preserved in the main line. This section may be only one or two pages of coding.
2. All other routines are written as though they were subroutines. These would include calculations, table look-ups, error routines, special tests, etc.

Although these will be written as subroutines, they do not precisely fall within the general definition of a subroutine, that is, a routine that is used by different parts of the program. This is not the case in modular programming. The program is broken up into these segments *only* for the purposes of clarity. It has no particular advantage in efficiency in the use of memory. It does, however, have the following advantages:

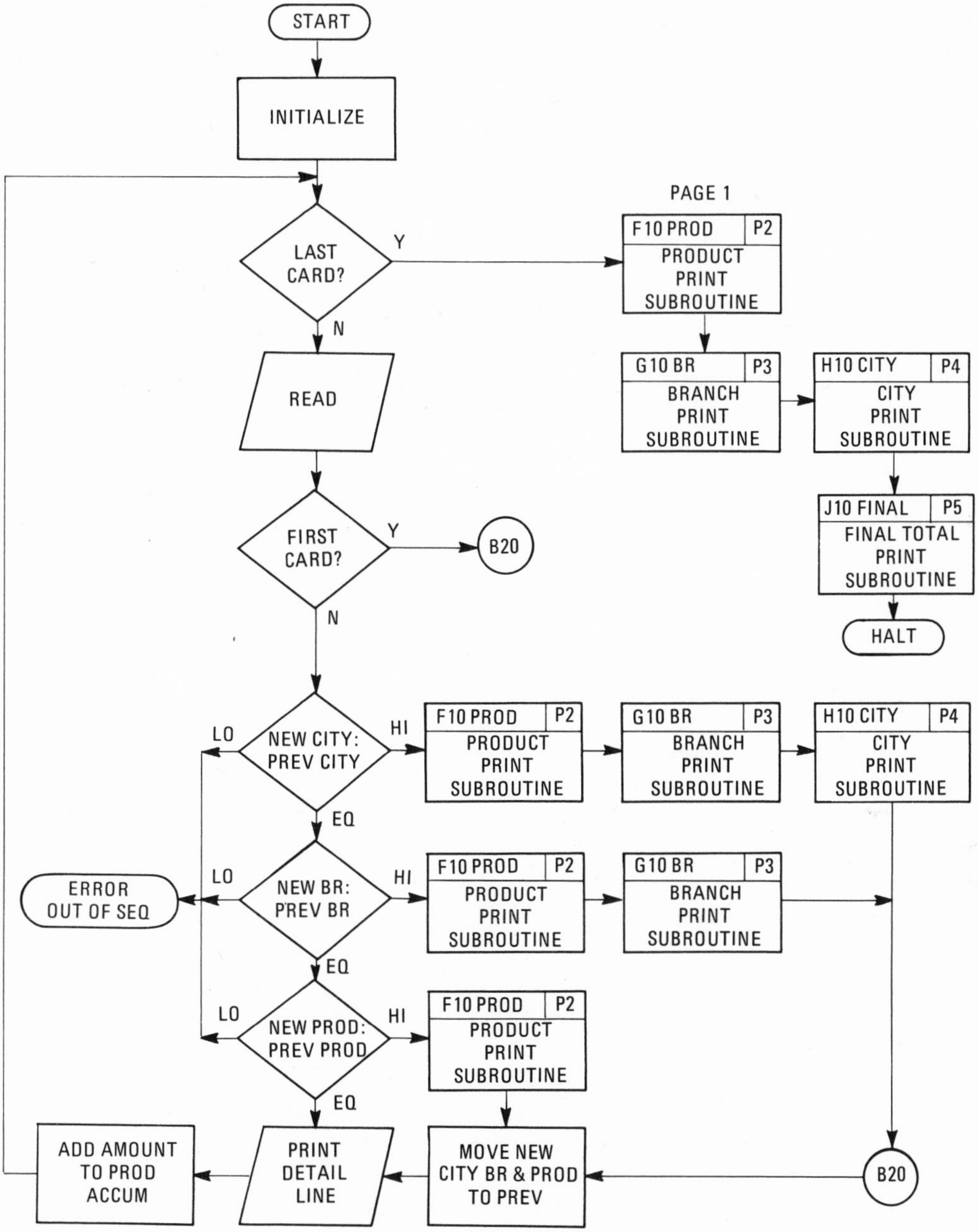

Fig. 9-4. Multilevel Control Break Using Subroutines.

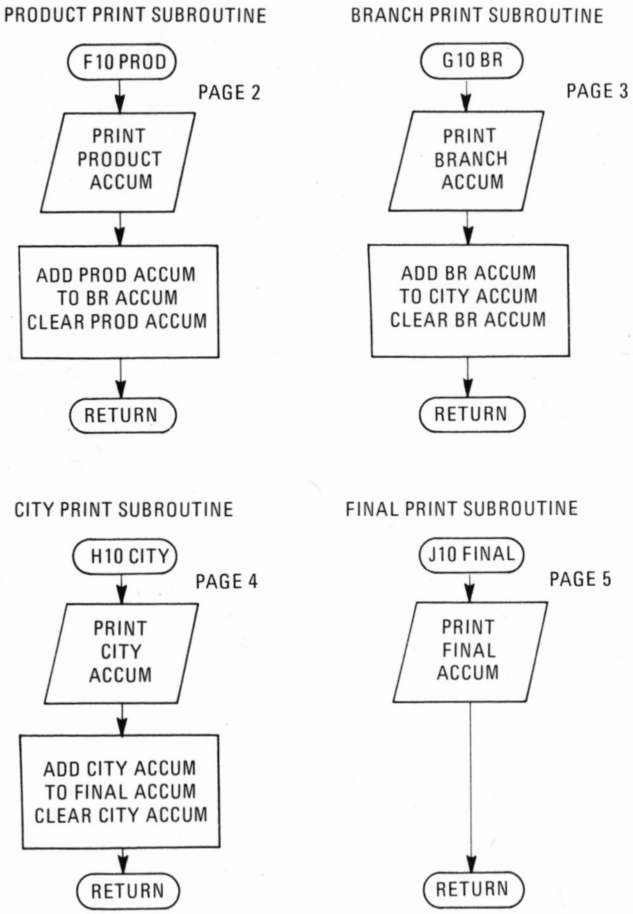

Fig. 9-5.

1. The programmer can better organize his thinking around the main structure of the program. It will force him to keep in the front of his mind the main line of the program and to keep the various more complicated but less relevant routines separate.
2. It enables teams of programmers to work on a project. Different programmers may be assigned various subroutines, and these subroutines may be compiled and debugged separately.
3. It permits easier legibility for others who subsequently will have to learn the program.

PROBLEMS

PROBLEM 9-1

What are the advantages (if any) of using subroutines? Under what conditions would you use (or not use) this technique?

PROBLEM 9-2

Sales Analysis

REQUIRED

Using Problem 4-2, redraw the flowchart.

1. Provide for page overflows as subroutines.
2. Draw the flowchart so that control breaks are handled as subroutines.

10

Input and Output Controls

Prior to the acceptance of data by the computer, considerable checking (or pre-editing) is generally required to be done. As a rule, the more important the input information, the more it will be checked and balanced by the various programs in the system.

Reasons for checking of the input are:

1. There may have been initial coding or transcribing errors in the source documents.
2. There may be keypunched errors in the cards. It is to be noted here that the keypunched card is usually also key-verified. In spite of this added precaution, however, keypunch errors are not always caught. Also, occasionally an error that is caught is incorrectly changed.
3. Cards may be lost or damaged in the system.
4. Cards may be missorted or misfiled.

It can be seen, therefore, that there is no reason to believe that the input data are necessarily valid, complete, or even in sequence. As will be seen in the following section, there are many items that may be checked by the program before the input is accepted as valid.

An important rule of data processing will be emphasized here.

Rule

All input records are pre-edited and checked for accuracy of totals by the computer before they are ever sorted.

The reason for this measure is that if the cards are sorted before they are pre-edited and totaled, then it is difficult, if not almost impossible, to locate errors. If the pre-editing program finds an erroneous total condition, it is necessary to compare the program listing against the original source documents. If they are not in the same sequence, then it is difficult to locate the error. After the records have been thoroughly verified by the computer and are considered acceptable, they may then be sorted into the required sequence for further processing.

TYPES OF ERROR CHECKING

Character Checking

It is sometimes necessary to check that a certain card column contains a specified type of punch. For instance, we may check for a particular card code and reject the card if it does not agree. The particular card code confirms that the card is a particular type of record.

Numeric Fields

Some card fields must be wholly numeric, such as account number, part number, and department. Each column of these fields can be examined to ensure that it contains only digits 0-9. This procedure, which can be performed more readily in a low-level language, is not always done. It may, however, be used where the information in the field is of critical importance. In this case, the programming time and effort may be worthwhile.

Alphabetic Fields

Pure alphabetic fields containing only the letters A-Z are occasionally encountered. Customer or employee names would be an example. Since these fields are usually maintained in a permanent master file, there is generally little purpose in repeatedly checking their validity.

Alphameric Fields

A field that may contain either numeric or alphabetic information is, for example, an address. Because of the variety of possible characters, such fields are difficult to check.

Note that amount fields which are purely numeric may have an "X" punch in the units position to denote a minus or credit amount. The units position in the field may then contain a multipunch similar to an alphabetic character. It should be kept in mind that because of reversing entries in the books of account, all amounts may be either positive or negative.

Sequence Checking

As a rule, the data will be in some predetermined sequence. It is not sufficient, however, to assume in the program that the cards are already in that sequence. There must always be a check to ensure that they are still in the proper order.

Special Tests

There are a number of tests that may be made that are unique to the particular card design or to an application:

1. Test for blanks. Most card designs contain columns that are unused. These columns may be checked to ensure that they are blank. Although this procedure may seem unnecessary, it is a wise precaution. If there is a punch in an unused column, this is a signal that something could be wrong with the card. A common cause of this error is "off-punching." The keypunch operator may have, for example, omitted punching one column and punched all the remaining data on the card one column to the left.
2. Reasonableness check. An amount field of either dollars or quantity may be examined to see if it is "reasonable." What is reasonable is a judgment of the programmer or analyst based on experience. A program for a telephone utility company may check that the number and charges for long-distance phone calls for a domestic customer were, based on historical records,

reasonable. If the fields exceed the estimated critical values, some specified action is to be taken. Also, the customer's consumption of electricity for the month is often checked for reasonableness by the electric utility company.

3. Limit check. There may be constant amounts determined by company policy or legal requirements that cannot be exceeded. For example, company policy dictates that net pay on a paycheck may not exceed $1000.00. Also, a previous problem gave an example of a customer's credit limit that may not be exceeded. Legal requirements may stipulate, for example, that the interest rate on borrowers' loans may not exceed 15% per annum.
4. Range check. This check applies to fields that are defined within a given range of numbers or characters. For example, in the payroll problem (Problem 7-2) that contains a code for job number, it may be that the range of possible codes extends from 06 to 75. All fields coded with numbers outside this range are recognized as invalid. Also, a field designated as a numeric month may be checked to ensure that the month coded is not less than 01 or greater than 12.

CORRECTIVE ACTION

When an error condition is encountered, certain action must be taken. This action will be determined by department policy and by the seriousness of the error. Although there are no hard and fast rules, three levels of errors may be considered:

1. Not serious. Accept the data but print a warning message. For example, the fact that a customer has exceeded his credit limit is no reason to reject the data. A message should be printed providing customer number, name, current balance, and credit limit so that the credit department may take any necessary action.
2. Fairly serious. Reject the data but print a warning message and continue processing. For example, an invalid card code may be encountered in a run. Department policy may decide that this type of error is not sufficiently serious to interrupt processing.
3. Serious. Print an error message and terminate the run. Generally, when a report is being produced, an out-of-sequence error is serious. For example, customers' accounts receivable are being updated, and the cards are discovered to be out of sequence. There will be incorrect totals for some customers, and possibly for departments as well. Restart procedures will be determined by the application being run and the computer hardware being used.

CONTROLS AND BALANCING

One of the most vital areas in data processing is that of balancing and controls. It is necessary that every program in the system contains checks that:

1. A file is in sequence.
2. The cards are for the correct file.
3. The total number of cards, quantities, and amounts are correct.

There are a number of considerations in checking for correct balances. The problem in any given program is, first, what are the relevant fields for balancing, and, second, what do we balance these fields to? It is the programmer's responsibility to ensure that he finds out which fields are to be used for balancing and to include these in the program.

As a general rule, totals are required for dollar amounts. An additional control aid is to keep the total number of input and output records. Occasionally, totals by quantity are also kept.

Batch Totals

Once cards are keypunched, they are checked and balanced *in their original sequence* by the pre-editing program. Since the cards are *not sorted* into some predetermined sequence, there is a problem in taking totals according to control levels. Although final totals may be easily obtained, these are not sufficient to trace out-of-balance conditions. What is required is a means of obtaining lower-level totals.

One technique commonly used is to have the source documents gathered in "batches." A batch may be constituted by the documents punched by a particular keypunch operator, by all the cards punched in a specified interval of time, or by a specified number of cards. The number of cards in a batch should be small enough that an error can easily be traced but large enough that the total number of batches is reasonable. A typical number might be between 30 and 100 cards. A manual total of dollars and number of entries is taken *from the source documents* for each batch. These figures are then punched on a "batch control card" that has its own unique card code and batch number. This card is inserted either before or after the given batch of cards. (Generally the batch control card is a different color and has a different corner cut in order to facilitate later separating of cards by batch.) In the computer balancing run, the totals of the batch of cards are subtracted from the totals in the batch control card. Since the totals should be equal, the difference should "zero-balance." The batch number and the difference are printed for audit trail purposes.

Balancing the Report

There are two chief sources of balancing or control totals.

Balance Forward Totals. These are last month's master file totals that are recorded in a data-processing control book. For instance, total accounts receivable as of the end of the previous month was $132,000. This figure will be this month's expected input balancing total. The programs that read in accounts receivable master cards will sum up this figure and print it out at the end of the report for balancing purposes. This amount will then be checked for agreement with that in the control book.

Current Entry Totals. This is activity during the current period, say, daily, weekly, or monthly. The control figures are usually included along with the source documents that are keypunched. When the keypunched cards are balanced on the computer (in their unsorted original sequence), the program will provide the required totals. These totals will be checked for agreement with the figures provided with the source documents. These amounts are recorded in the control book.

Ideally, as many totals should be recorded as are practically possible. Too many totals can be cumbersome and time-consuming, but there should be enough to ensure that the file is still valid and intact and that errors may be traced readily. The totals that should be kept depend on the number of control fields and the number of amounts being carried.

We have discussed in earlier chapters multilevel control breaks. In this type of program, totals are taken for every level–minor, intermediate, major, and final totals. For example, a program produces a report of sales that includes, as well as other detail, amounts for gross sales, cost of goods sold, and gross profit. Further, the control fields are minor, salesman; intermediate, department; and major, store. The total of gross sales, cost of sales, and gross profit will be printed for each salesman, for each department, for each store, and for final totals (see Figure 10-1).

Sales Analysis Report – 31 August 19XX

STORE	DEPT	SALESMAN		GROSS SALES	COST OF SALES	GROSS PROFIT
1	1	3	J B SMITH	20,600.00	14,500.00	6,100.00
1	1	5	S A JONES	28,200.00	18,400.00	9,800.00
TOTAL DEPT 1				48,800.00	32,900.00	15,900.00 *
1	2	2	P R JACKSON	8,200.00	6,100.00	2,100.00
1	2	8	A MCKAY	18,700.00	13,600.00	5,100.00
TOTAL DEPT 2				26,900.00	19,700.00	7,200.00 *
TOTAL STORE 1				75,700.00	52,600.00	23,100.00 **
2	1	4	J R PRESTON	19,500.00	14,000.00	5,500.00
2	1	9	D BOGLE	25,800.00	16,700.00	9,100.00
TOTAL DEPT 1				45,300.00	30,700.00	14,600.00 *
TOTAL STORE 2				45,300.00	30,700.00	14,600.00 **
FINAL TOTAL				121,000.00	83,300.00	37,700.00 ***

Fig. 10-1.

The purposes of producing all of these totals are:

1. The information may be required by sales managers.
2. Some of these totals may be required as entries in the company's general ledger.
3. The totals are necessary to ensure that the report is in balance. If the final total is not in balance with the data-processing records, then the control clerk can check the store totals to determine which store is out of balance. He may then check the department totals to determine which of these is out of balance. In this fashion he may quickly locate the error condition.

Another example discussed earlier is that of file updating. In this type of application, there are two or more types of input cards. The master file will be balanced against last month's totals, whereas the transaction file will be balanced against the current entries recorded in the control book. It is necessary that the program provide the totals of both master and transaction cards.

For example, consider an accounts receivable update. Control fields are minor, customer number, and major, store number. The master card contains the customer's balance as of the end of the previous month. One type of transaction card contains customer sales for the current month and another type of transaction card contains current payments. The report should provide, then, as well as other details for each customer, previous balance, current sales, current payments, and new balance. Totals by customer and store and final totals should be printed for each of these amounts (see Figure 10-2).

Customers' Accounts Updating – 31 August 19XX

STORE		*CUSTOMER*	*PREV BALANCE*	*SALES*	*PAYTS*	*NEW BALANCE*
1	12	A C CHURN	1,200.00	500.00	150.00	1,550.00
1	15	K R HOLDEN	100.00 -	200.00	120.00	20.00 -
1	22	R P MCGAVIN	500.00	100.00 -	30.00	370.00
TOTAL STORE 1			1,600.00	600.00	300.00	1,900.00 *
2	8	F N SENOUR	650.00	0.00	50.00 -	700.00
2	11	M R SCREEVE	1,050.00	200.00	0.00	1,250.00
TOTAL STORE 2			1,700.00	200.00	50.00 -	1,950.00 *
FINAL TOTAL			3,300.00	800.00	250.00	3,850.00 **

Fig. 10-2.

This report may be balanced as follows: Total previous balance may be checked for agreement with the total as of the end of the previous month recorded in the control book. Both total sales and payments may be checked for agreement with the totals for the current month. The total new balance, if correct, will be recorded in the control book and will be next month's previous balance. If any of these figures do not agree, then the control clerk can check the totals by store and then by customer to determine where the error occurred.

DATE CARDS

A useful device used in many installations is the date card. The date card will contain a specified card code and possibly both a numeric date, such as 08 31 1971 (or 31 08 1971), and an alphabetic date, August 31, 1971. A date card will precede each set of data cards fed into the system. The program is written so that at its initialization it will read a card, check that the card is a date card, and then store the date in some preassigned area in core. (The program may also check that the date as read was valid. For example, the numeric month must be 01 to 12 and the day may not exceed 31.)

For a computer run that pre-edits and balances keypunched cards, the date on the date card will generally be "today's" date. For programs that produce a report, the date card will generally contain, not today's date, but rather the date for which the report is effective, e.g., the last day of the preceding month.

Date cards have two purposes.

1. Printing the date on the report.
2. For control purposes. In this case the program may use the date card to check that the input cards contain the valid month. For example, consider the accounts receivable update report mentioned earlier. The date card will contain 08 31 1971.

Checking of input will be as follows:

1. All transactions cards—sales and payments—must contain the *current* month, 08.
2. All master cards must contain the *preceding* month, 07. Note that if the current month is January (01), then the preceding month will be December (12).

Date checks used as described above are particularly useful in detecting card-handling errors. First, an operator can supply transaction cards for the wrong month, say those of July instead of August. Second, he can supply master cards for the wrong month, say June instead of July. In either case, without a date card check, the error possibly would not be caught until the operator attempts to balance the control totals after the run is completed.

Summary

—Anything that can go wrong (in data processing) will go wrong.
—In every computer run, the data must be checked and balanced.
—Once cards are keypunched, they must be pre-edited in the sequence in which they were punched. In this pre-editing run, every possible check is performed—sequence, card codes, limit checks, reasonableness, etc. Totals are printed and balanced with the source documents.
—In all other processing runs, the input does not require such extensive checking. It is still necessary, however, to check at least for sequence, card codes, and totals. Other checks will depend on the application. Totals are printed for all levels of control and for all amount fields.
—Printed control totals for all runs are balanced with the data-processing control book before any further processing is done.
—The use of date cards in all runs provides an additional useful data-processing control.

Thorough checking and balancing of data will minimize errors in data processing. It is, however, no guarantee that the data are absolutely valid. There are some errors that programming can never catch. At the time the source document is written, the wrong part number or quantity may be entered. At keypunch time, source documents may be mislaid, or errors in punching may be missed. During the program run, an operator may neglect to act on error messages, may fail to balance the printed report to the control book, or may fail to check that balance forward cards punched do balance to the correct total.

ELEMENTS OF GOOD REPORT DESIGN

The study of controls and balances leads now to consideration of how they should be presented on the computer report. This area is very broad, however, and its details are better left to the field of systems analysis. This book will cover only the minimum presentation necessary for a programmer.

Continuous forms are supplied in a variety of widths and lengths, although certain sizes such as 15 X 11 inches have become fairly standardized. In addition to single-part forms, carbon inserts permit the use of forms that are two-part, three-part, and more.

Other than size and number of copies, forms may be divided into two general categories. The first is the preprinted form. According to data-processing specifications, the form supplier will print these forms with headings and vertical lines to separate the fields. This type of form is generally used for documents sent outside the company, such as customer bills and employee checks. The advantages of preprinted forms are

1. Since less printing of headings is required by the computer, there is a saving in time and memory storage.
2. These reports are generally neat and easy to read.
3. Maximum use of the printer width is possible. With vertical lines we are able to place amount fields adjacent to each other. There is no need for spaces to separate these fields.

The other common type of form is "stock tab." This form contains no special printing but has instead only horizontal lines or stripes. This type of form is generally used for editing and balancing and for reports distributed within the company. The advantages of this type of form are

1. They are less expensive than preprinted forms.
2. Since they do not require a special order, the supplier can print and deliver them with less delay.
3. Since the report is not locked into a specifically designed form, the report may be changed merely by amending the program.

We will concern ourselves here with the stock tab form and the typical report layout as normally designed by the programmer. These report formats should be standardized for all programmers in an installation. The prime factors in good report design are as follows:

1. Headings. If the report is to remain within the company, it is only necessary to print the company name on the first page, if even there.

   The number of lines of heading should be kept at a *minimum*. Much time and forms space are wasted in the needless printing of trivial headings at the top of each page.

   Headings should be clear and concise.

   Each heading should contain a date and page number on every page.

   Some installations require that, for purposes of ready identification, the program number is printed in the heading.

   Control fields should be printed with the major field to the left and minor fields to the right (see Figure 10-1).

   Updating reports should be printed with the previous balance on the left, then transactions, and then the new balance on the right (see Figure 10-2).
2. Detail lines. All *relevant* information should be included. Since it takes (normally) no longer to use every print position than to use only half of them, consider printing all data that could be of use. The programmer, however, must provide a neat, uncluttered report.

   Amount fields should be sufficiently large to accommodate the largest possible amount that could *ever* be expected to appear.

   Amount fields should always provide for negatives, using either the CR or – symbol.

   Amounts generally should be programmed by moving and editing them from *right* to left. (This rule is more specific to the language being used. In 360 Assembler language, for example, there is a "fill character" at the left of the edit word. If the amount fields are adjacent to each other, the fill character will erase the rightmost character of the field to the left if it has been previously moved and edited there.) Generally, all amount fields should be edited with leading blanks, commas, decimals, and credits. Dollar signs are not normally printed on reports but are used chiefly for printing checks and bills.
3. Totals. Totals for every amount field and for every control level should be printed.

   Total fields can be expected to be longer than detail fields.

Total fields should normally line up with detail according to the *units* position (see Figure 10-1).

Intermediate and major totals may be printed directly under the minor total (see Figure 4-2) or offset a full field to the right (see Figure 4-4).

The normal convention for depicting levels of control totals is through the use of asterisks. Minor totals will have one asterisk, intermediate two, and major three.

Totals that cannot fit on a single line under the detail may be "staggered." Final totals in Figure 10-2 could be staggered as follows:

```
3300.00              250.00-
          800.00               3,850.00 **
```

4. Page overflow. There are various ways of determining when the "bottom" of the page has been reached. One common method is to use a count of the number of lines on a page. This number will be determined by the length of the form, the number of lines of headings, etc. Details of programming this technique are covered in the chapter on subroutines.

   Print the page number on each page.

   Provide sufficient space for the possible printing of totals at the bottom of the page. It is more desirable to print these totals beneath the detail on the same page rather than at the top of the following page.

   At the end of a control break, such as for a branch, the totals for the previous branch are printed. If a copy of the report is sent to the branch, it will be necessary at this point for the program to skip to a new page to begin printing the next branch.

   In this case also, final totals will be printed at the end on a separate page. In this way the totals of all branches will not be included on the copy sent to the last branch. Further, the branch number should be printed in the *heading* of each page rather than listed down one side. This practice will make for a neater report and will provide additional print space on each line.

PROBLEMS

PROBLEM 10-1

What action should the program take when it encounters an out-of-sequence condition? What factors influence this decision?

PROBLEM 10-2

Refer to Problem 4-2. Why would we require totals of sales amount by salesman, district, and division? What particular employees would want these totals?

PROBLEM 10-3

For how many periods do you think it would be necessary to store an "old" file of inventory master cards? Of monthly transaction cards?

PROBLEM 10-4

In an inventory update run such as Problem 3-3, why would we always print totals of old balance, of receipts, of issues, and of new balance?

PROBLEM 10-5

What is the advantage of assigning a field on the input records for month or period? Is the period on the transaction card the same as on the old master card in an update run?

PROBLEM 10-6

In a program producing an accounts receivable report by store, why will it be desirable to skip to a new page at the beginning of the data for each store? Why should each store start with page 1?

PROBLEM 10-7

A file of accounts payable cards contains

Supplier master cards (card code 41)–supplier number, name, address
Invoice transactions (card code 42)–supplier number, invoice number, date of invoice, amount billed

There are one master and any number of transactions per supplier.

1. After the cards have been keypunched, what tests and balances would you suggest be provided by the pre-edit program?
2. Once the file has been checked and accepted as valid, what tests and balances (if any) would you provide in subsequent programs that use this file to produce reports?

PROBLEM 10-8

After employee time cards have been keypunched and key verified, it is necessary to pre-edit and balance the cards on the computer. Refer to Problem 4-1 and write a program that will thoroughly check the time cards depicted in that problem. In addition to any other special pre-editing, check for the following:

1. Valid card code.
2. Valid store-department number. Set up a table of valid store-department numbers, from store 01 department 001 through store 46 department 516 as follows: 01001, 01006, 01014, . . . , 46516. Make up about forty entries. Check against the table to ensure that each time card has a valid store-department number.
3. Correct totals of hours. Assume that the cards are batched by store number with a control tape for each batch.
4. Valid month.
5. Valid job number. Set up a table of valid job numbers.
6. If hours exceed 70.0, print a query. Hours may be negative to permit reversing entries.
7. Rate must be positive and may not exceed $8.500.

Optional: Check that numeric fields contain only numeric data and employee name contains only alphabetic characters.

11

Special Topics

The principles given in previous chapters will be found applicable over and over again in many business programming applications. In addition, of course, there are more specialized techniques, sometimes invented by individual programmers for special needs. The following examples may be of interest and assistance in appropriate cases.

DIRECT TABLE ADDRESSING

This technique is applicable to the searching of sequential discrete-type tables where all possible arguments are valid. Consider, for example, the case of job numbers and rates of pay as in Chapter 7 (Figure 7-1) and assume that every job number from 00 to 99 is valid and has an associated rate.

By definition, job 00 is the first entry, job 01 is the second, job 02 is the third, and so on. Thus the search job number tells us exactly where to look for the appropriate table entry. Instead of having to search the table for a matching table job number by incrementing the COMPARE instruction and MULT instruction by 5 at a time, we can dispense with the COMPARE instruction and merely increment the MULT instruction by 5 times the job number. For example, job 02 is the third entry. The address of table argument 02 therefore is TAB + 5 + 5 or TAB + 2 X 5, and the address of the corresponding table function or rate is RATE + 2 X 5.

The PLC program would then be simplified to

LABEL	OPERATION	OPERAND	COMMENTS
	RESET	OPERAND 2 OF CALC TO 'RATE'	INITIALIZE THE TABLE
	MULT	SEARCH ARG BY '5'	
	ADD	PRODUCT TO OPERAND 2 OF CALC	PRODUCT = SEARCH ARG X 5
CALC	MULT	HRS BY RATE	

Notice that with this method the table arguments, i.e., the job numbers, are not used at all, and in fact are completely superfluous. They can, therefore, be omitted from the table in the memory and only the functions stored. However, in this case each table entry will consist of the rate only, and since this will occupy only three storage positions, the factor by which the SEARCH ARG is multiplied must be 3 instead of 5.

The rules for finding a function by direct addressing are

1. The table must consist only of entries for positive, consecutive, sequential arguments. The argument itself need not be included.
2. The address of the required function is calculated by
   Address of the table + (search argument X length of each entry in the table).
3. If the first table argument is greater than zero or the last table argument is less than the highest possible search argument, then special programming must accommodate these exceptions.

For example, suppose the only valid job numbers are those from 10 to 80. The program has to reject any search argument that is less than 10 or greater than 80. Then, by subtracting 10 from the valid search argument, we can calculate the address of the required function as in rule 2.

Note: The preceding discussion applies chiefly to low-level assembler languages. In high-level compiler languages such as Fortran and PL/I, the search argument may take the form of a "subscript" which points directly to the function in the table.

For example, consider a search argument called K and a table called TABLE. If K takes the value one, then TABLE(K) refers to the first entry. If K takes the value five, then TABLE(K) refers to the fifth entry. The compiler itself automatically calculates the address of the required function according to rule 2.

DECIMAL ACCUMULATION

Where a number of calculated results are accumulated to give a total, and where each result has been rounded or half-adjusted, it is possible for a small error to accumulate. In some cases this may cause a problem which can, however, be solved by special programming.

A common case is that of ratio or percentage calculations. Consider the following sales analysis figures for example.

PRODUCT	*AMOUNT SOLD ($)*	*RATIO TO TOTAL (6 DECIMALS)*	*HALF-ADJUSTED TO 1 DECIMAL (%)*	*DECIMAL ACCUMULATION*	*RESULT USING DECIMAL ACCUMULATION (%)*
101	1,262.25	0.112483	11.2	0.112983	11.2
102	237.62	0.021175	2.1	0.022158	2.2
105	117.00	0.010426	1.0	0.010584	1.0
112	9,521.18	0.848464	84.8	0.849048	84.9
114	83.61	0.007450	0.7	0.007498	0.7
	11,221.66	0.999998	99.8		100.0

The third column shows the ratio of sales of each product to the total sales to six decimal places. Simple rounding or half-adjusting gives the results shown in the fourth column. It will be noted that these do not add up to 100%. This is an undesirable feature of such a report.

The fifth column shows a technique for overcoming this difficulty. The 0.000500 required for rounding is added only once, at the beginning. However, unwanted digits in the last three decimal places at each calculation are not dropped but are added to the result of the next calculation.

The procedure, then, is as follows:

1. Initialize a decimal accumulator as 0.000500.
2. Add this to the first ratio (0.112483 + 0.000500 = 0.112983).
3. Store the unwanted digits (0.000983) back in the decimal accumulator. Store the 0.112 as the answer.
4. Calculate the next ratio and add the decimal accumulator to it (0.021175 + 0.000983 = 0.022158).
5. Store the unwanted digits (0.000158) in the decimal accumulator. Store the 0.022 as the answer.
6. Continue in this manner.

Another useful application of this technique is in allocation of expenses between departments or cost centers on a percentage basis. In this case the total of the individual expenses allocated must equal the total expense.

Cost Allocations

(1)	(2)	(3)	(4)	(5)	(6)
TOTAL EXPENSES TO BE ALLOCATED OVER COST CENTERS ($)	*COST CENTER*	*PERCENT TO BE ALLOCATED*	*CALCULATION (1) X (3) ($)*	*HALF-ADJUSTED TO 2 DECIMALS*	*RESULT USING DECIMAL ACCUMULATION ($)*
6,250.13	A	23.5	1468.78055	1468.78	1468.78
	B	16.2	1012.52106	1012.52	1012.52
	C	9.6	600.01248	600.01	600.01
	D	25.1	1568.78263	1568.78	1568.79
	E	25.6	1600.03328	1600.03	1600.03
	TOTAL	100.0	6250.13000	6250.12	6250.13

In this example, total costs of $6250.13 are to be allocated in the following fashion: 23.5% to cost center A, 16.2% to B, 9.6% to C, 25.1% to D, and 25.6% to E. $6250.13 should, therefore, be fully allocated.

The cost for each cost center (column 4) is determined by multiplying total expenses (column 1) by the cost center percent (column 3).

It can be seen that whereas the total cost allocated by simple half-adjusting is $6250.12, the use of decimal accumulation allocates the full $6250.13. Although the difference seems trivial, good cost accounting requires the full amount to be allocated.

Note The programmer is warned that if negative results are possible (e.g., through reversing entries), then additional programming will be required. Two decimal accumulators must be provided. One contains initially a positive 5 for use with positive results. The other contains initially a minus 5 for use with negative results. A test for the sign of the result must be made before the rounding process is carried out, and the appropriate decimal accumulator must be used.

SORTING

Occasionally, we may have data stored in memory in a tabular form but in a sequence which is not suitable for subsequent processing. [For instance, the job number and rate table (Figure 7-1) is not in the appropriate sequence for printing out the rates of pay in order of magnitude.] This situation may arise because the data were in suitable sequence for some previous process or report.

The problem of sorting these data into some other predetermined sequence is relatively simple, using a technique of successive comparisons and interchange of pairs of numbers.

The following table shows scores made by students in a quiz. These are stored in the memory in random sequence (possibly they were originally read in student number sequence). The maximum mark is 100, so that each entry is three positions long.

Entry	*Score*
1	064
2	086
3	057
4	038
5	091
6	073
7	077

We require that the scores be sorted into ascending sequence. The basis of the technique is

1. Search through the table to find the lowest number and interchange it with the first entry.
2. Search for the next lowest number and interchange it with the second entry.
3. Continue in this manner throughout the table.

Following this procedure, we compare the first entry in the table (064) with the second entry (086). 064 is lower so we proceed to the third entry (057). This is lower than 064 so we interchange the two numbers, leaving 057 as the first entry and 064 as the third.

We now continue to compare the first entry (which is now 057) against the fourth (038) and again make an exchange. 038 becomes the first entry and 057 the fourth.

Continuing now to compare the first entry (038) with the remaining entries we find no further exchanges necessary. We know, therefore, that the first entry in the table now contains the lowest score and need not be considered in subsequent processing.

The table at this point reads

Entry	*Score*
1	038
2	086
3	064
4	057
5	091
6	073
7	077

We now repeat the process, starting with the second entry (086). We compare this with the third entry, 064, which is lower, and so an exchange occurs. Next a comparison of 064 with 057 results in another exchange. Subsequent comparisons leave 057 as the second entry.

We continue in this fashion until we have the sixth lowest number stored as the sixth entry. The sort may then be terminated since the seventh entry will contain the highest score.

Figure 11-1 provides a general flowchart solution of this procedure.

CALCULATING NUMBER OF DAYS BETWEEN DATES

Occasionally a problem arises in which it is necessary to calculate how many days have elapsed between two dates. Quite often, for example, such a calculation is required for determining interest on loans. Now, if the customer last made a payment on June 10 and his

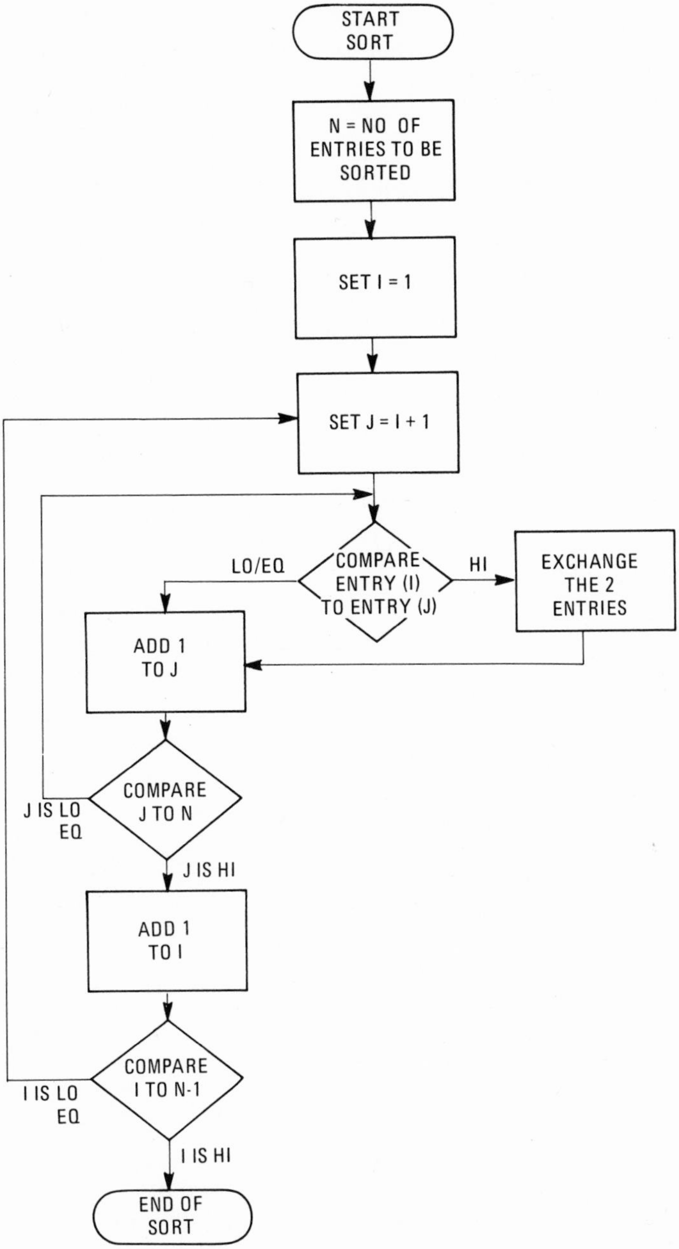

Fig. 11-1. Sort Flowchart.

next payment is July 15, then it is not too difficult to determine mentally that the number of days between these two dates equals 20 for June plus 15 for July, giving 35. However, how would we program a computer such that the calculation is generalized for any dates of the calendar?

The procedure to follow requires that we calculate what number day of the year each of the dates falls upon. June 10, for example, is the 161st day of the year and July 15 is the 196th day of the year. It is easy to see that the difference between these two days of the year gives us the same number of days that we calculated before, that is, 35.

The only problem now is how to set up days of the year. One way would be to establish a table of 365 entries beginning with a table argument containing month and day–that is, January 1, January 2, etc.–and the function containing the day of the year–1, 2, etc. The table would terminate with December 31 containing the function 365. Such a table would be unduly long and would require an unnecessarily large amount of memory as well as considerable time required for table look-up.

A simpler table is one in which there is a table argument for the month only, while the function contains the accumulated days of the year up to that month. The table is listed below:

Month	*Accumulated Days*
01	000
02	031
03	059
04	090
05	120
06	151
07	181
08	212
09	243
10	273
11	304
12	334

What we have to do in order to find the day of the year is, using table look-up, locate the correct month and use the function as the accumulated days to date. (Direct addressing may be used.) In the case of July, the function is 181. Add the day of the month to the function that we have extracted: 181 plus 15 equals 196.

Repeating this procedure for June 10 we get 151 plus 10 equals

161. The days between the two calculated days of the year is then 196 - 161 = 35.

A minor problem arises when the days overlap a year end. For example, the current date could be February 3, while the preceding date was December 19. The difference between these two dates is 034 minus 353 equals -319. When we cross the year end we have to make an adjustment of 365 days. By adding 365 to -319 we will obtain the correct answer of 46 days.

The programmer will have to check whether he has crossed over one or two or more years in calculating the difference between dates.

A further awkward situation arises because of leap years. The additional day for February 29 is not accounted for in the table. Extra programming will be required to allow for this situation. It is always possible to determine that a given year is a leap year by the fact that it is evenly divisible by 4 (i.e., there will be zero remainder). The exception to this rule is any year ending with 00 such as 1900, 2000, unless the first two digits are evenly divisible by four.

BINARY SEARCH

The method given for table searching in Chapter 7 is straightforward but very inefficient for large tables. If we were to search for a number in the telephone directory by such a technique (i.e., starting at the first entry and continuing to inspect each one until we came to the one we wanted), business would come to a standstill.

Thus, taking as an example the table of job numbers and assuming all possible numbers 00-99 are used, it would take on the average 50 comparisons to find the desired entry.

Now each comparison involves at least 5 instructions so that on the average each data card will require the execution of 250 instructions to find the appropriate entry.

The technique known as *binary search* will reduce this number considerably.

The principle used is to start the search at the *middle* of the table instead of the beginning and find out in which half of the table the desired entry lies. The process is then repeated on this half and so on, thus zeroing in quite rapidly on the correct entry.

For purposes of illustration, we shall use a table with only 20 entries (Figure 11-2).

Entry Number	*Job Number*	*Rate*
1	01	3.25
2	02	4.15
3	04	4.25
4	07	5.15
5	13	3.85
6	15	4.15
7	21	4.25
8	27	4.15
9	30	4.65
10	47	2.75
11	50	4.15
12	51	4.25
13	56	4.85
14	62	4.75
15	67	4.15
16	69	4.25
17	75	4.15
18	76	4.75
19	78	4.95
20	99	0.00

Fig. 11-2. Job Number and Rate of Pay Table.

To find the middle entry, we take the first and last entry numbers, i.e., 1 and 20 and average them:

$$\frac{1 + 20}{2} = 10\tfrac{1}{2}$$

Obviously we cannot have an entry 10½, so by convention we truncate and take the tenth entry.

We will start searching, then, at the *tenth* entry, which is job 47.

If we compare the search argument with this we find out one of three things:

1. If the search argument equals the table argument, we have found the required entry.
2. If the search argument is lower than the table argument, we know that the required entry is in the lower half of the table.
3. If the search argument is higher than the table argument, the required entry is in the upper half of the table.

For example, if the input card contains job 21, we will find that this is lower than 47 so we have immediately eliminated the upper half of the table. Let us now take the entry at the middle of the lower half, i.e., we compute (1 + 10)/2 = 5½, giving us entry 5 or job 13.

Comparing 21 to 13 we find a high comparison so we know now that the desired entry is in the second quarter of the table.

We must now find the midpoint of this quarter of the table, i.e., the seventh entry. [(5 + 10)/2 = 7½].

Since the job number of entry 7 happens to be 21, the next comparison shows that we have found the correct entry.

To illustrate further, suppose the search argument is 69. Starting at entry 10 we find at once that the required entry is in the upper half of the table. We have, therefore, saved searching the first 9 entries in the table. If this had been a 100-entry table, we would have saved 49 searches with our first test.

We now have to find the midpoint of the upper half of the table. This is the (10 + 20)/2 = 15 entry, which is job 67. The comparison gives a high result so we go to the next midpoint, which is the seventeenth entry [(15 + 20)/2 = 17½]. This is job 75 and we now get a low comparison. Therefore, we must now take the midpoint between this entry and the preceding entry tested, which was 15. The midpoint is (17 + 15)/2 = 16. The argument for entry 16 is 69 and so we have found the desired entry.

Developing the Flowchart

Summarizing the steps in the last example, we have the following procedure:

	LO		*HI*
Consider the range of entries from	1	to	20
Midpoint is		10	
Comparison with entry 10 gives *high* compare		↙	
Therefore, now consider the range of entries from	10	to	20
Midpoint is		15	
Comparison with entry 15 gives *high* compare		↙	

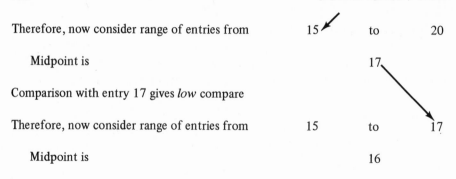

Therefore, now consider range of entries from	15	to	20
Midpoint is		17	
Comparison with entry 17 gives *low* compare			
Therefore, now consider range of entries from	15	to	17
Midpoint is		16	
Comparison with entry 16 gives *equal* compare			
Search completed			

Notice that when the compare is high, the previous *low* entry is replaced by the old midpoint to find the new midpoint. When the compare is low, the previous *high* entry is replaced. Hence the flowchart shown in Figure 11-3 will meet our requirements, *provided there is a matching entry in the table for the search argument.*

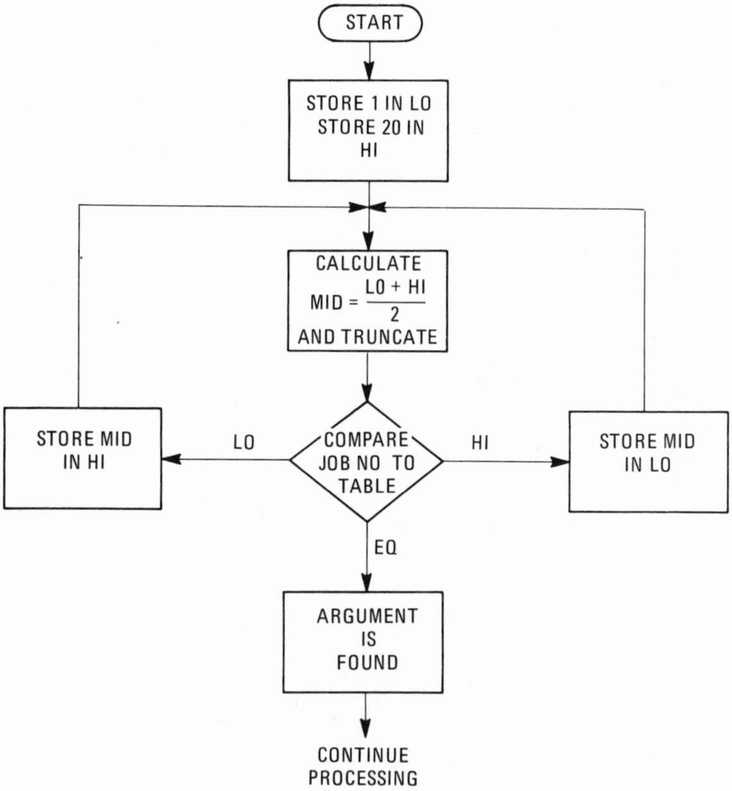

Fig. 11-3. Binary Search Table Look-up (No Missing Entries).

Missing Entries

We must now consider the case where we have a search argument with no matching table argument. We cannot use the method given in Chapter 7 where a low comparison signaled a missing entry since we are not proceeding uniformly through the table.

Let us consider an example using the job number table with an input record of job 20, which is not in the table. The search will proceed as follows:

		LO		*HI*
Range		1		20
Midpoint			10	
Comparison of 20 : 47	low			
Range		1		10
Midpoint			5	
Comparison of 20 : 13	high			
Range		5		10
Midpoint			7	
Comparison of 20 : 21	low			
Range		5		7
Midpoint			6	
Comparison of 20 : 15	high			
Range		6		7
Midpoint			6	
Comparison of 20 : 15	high			
Range		6		7
Midpoint			6	

.
.
.

Note that after a time we start repeating the comparison of the search argument with the identical table argument, i.e., entry 6. This can be used as a simple test to check that an entry is not in the table. The flowchart is shown in Figure 11-4. The student should check out further examples to satisfy himself that this technique will work in all cases.

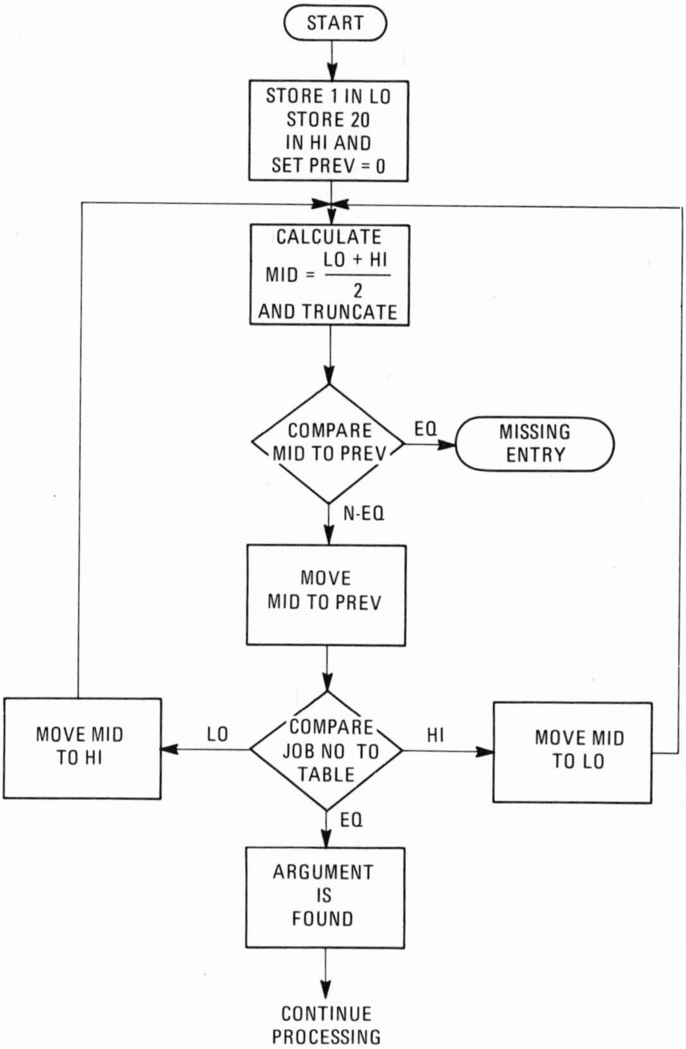

Fig. 11-4. Binary Search Table Look-up (Missing Entries).

PROBLEMS

PROBLEM 11-1 (mandatory)

Mortgage Interest Calculation

OBJECTIVE

To calculate the interest and principal on mortgages. By applying current payments to mortgages, calculate the interest, the amount applied to principal, and the new balance of the mortgage.

INPUT

1. Mortgage master (1 card per account):

	COLUMN
Card code (21)	1-2
Mortgage number	3-7
Name of mortgagee	8-27
Date mortgage issued (dd mm yy)	33-38
Rate of interest (.XXXX)	39-42 (0.0625 = 6.25%)
Original balance (XXXXX.XX)	43-49
Current balance (XXXXX.XX)	55-61
Date of last payment (dd mm yy)	62-67

2. Payment (1 card per account):

	COLUMN
Card code (22)	1-2
Mortgage number	3-7
Payment amount (XXX.XX). Can be negative	50-54
Current date (dd mm yy)	62-67

PROCEDURE

1. Days = current date - date of last payment.
2. Interest = (days/365) X rate X current balance.
3. New balance = old balance - (payment - interest).
4. Treat the "days" table look-up as a subroutine.
5. Provide for page overflow subroutine.

OUTPUT

Print a report showing all relevant information concerning the mortgage account, balances, rate, dates, etc., used in the calculation.

Provide the necessary final control totals.

Test cards should provide for

1. Negative days between dates—an error

2. Negative new balance
3. Negative payments (adjustments)

PROBLEM 11-2

Direct Table Addressing

OBJECTIVE

To store in a table, by code, data read randomly from punched cards and to output totals by code at the end of the run.

INPUT

	COLUMN
Card code (06)	1-2
Model code (0-9)	5
Amount (XXXX.XX)	11-16

PROCEDURE

Set up a table in core in the following fashion:

Model Code 0 No. Amt Descrip'n FORD	Model Code 1 No. Amt Descrip'n MUSTANG	Model Code 2 No. Amt Descrip'n MERCURY

— — — — — — — —	Model Code 9 No. Amt Descrip'n T-BIRD

The cards are read in *random* sequence. The amount on the card is to be added to the table according to the *model code* on the card. A 1 is to be added to the number of entries for that code.

Do not test the model code. Instead, use the model code to modify the instruction that adds into the table.

OUTPUT

At the end of the run, output the totals as shown. Omit output for model codes that have no entries.

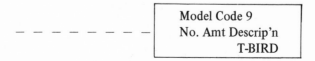

Used Car Sales, April 1972

CODE	*DESCRIP'N*	*NO.*	*AMT. ($)*
0	FORD	1	50.00
1	MUSTANG	1	700.00

Used Car Sales, April 1972 (Continued)

CODE	*DESCRIP'N*	*NO.*	*AMT. ($)*
2	MERCURY	2	350.00
	.		
	.		
	.		
9	T-BIRD	2	1250.00
		6 *	2350.00 *

REQUIRED

Completely tested and documented program.

PROBLEM 11-3

Decimal Accumulation

Revise your program for Problem 7-2 to include a *percentage* distribution of wages by department as well as the actual wages distribution. Use decimal accumulation to ensure that the total adds up to 100%. Also use *binary search* for the table look-up procedure.

PROBLEM 11-4

Sorting of Data in Core and Statistical Calculation

INPUT

Applicants for employment have written an aptitude test. Their scores are punched 10 to a card:

1-2	3-5	6-8	9-11	12-14	15-17	18-20	21-23	24-26	27-29	30-32
08	XXX	XXX	XXX	XXX	XXX	XXX	XXX	XXX	XXX	XXX
	(1)	(2)	(3)	(4)	(5)	(6)	(7)	(8)	(9)	(10)
CARD CODE					*TEST SCORES*					

PROCEDURE

The test scores are to be stored consecutively in a table in core. The scores from the first card will be stored in the first 10 fields, those from the second card in the eleventh to twentieth fields, etc. Provide for a maximum of 25 cards (or 250 scores).

Count the number of scores stored. *Note:* the *last* card does not necessarily contain 10 scores, but all others must.

After the cards have been stored, *sort* the scores in the table into ascending sequence.

Calculate the *mean score:*

$$\text{Mean} = \frac{\text{sum of scores}}{\text{number of scores}}$$

Calculate the *standard deviation* (where n is the total number of scores and x is the value of the scores):

$$s = \sqrt{\frac{n(\Sigma x^2) - (\Sigma x)^2}{n(n-1)}}$$

OUTPUT

Calculate and print the number of applicants and the *variance* for each score (variance = score − mean).

Provide for headings and page numbering.

Statistical Report

NO	*SCORE*	*VARIANCE*
1	36	13.0-
3	38	11.0-
13	41	8.0-
	.	.
	.	.
	.	.
2	72	23.0

MEAN = 49.0 STANDARD DEVIATION = 7.52

Optional: Calculate and print the median score.

Appendix A

Coding of Job Number and Pay Rate Table Look-up†

1. 1620 SPS Using Address Modification

	SYMBOLIC		*MACHINE LANGUAGE*			
	TFM	TEST+11,TAB	00402	16	00437	$\bar{0}$0606
	TFM	CALC+11,RATE	00414	16	00509	$\bar{0}$0609
TEST	C	JOBIN,TAB	00426	24	00601	00606
	BL	ERROR	00438	47	XXXXX	01300
	BE	CALC	00450	46	00498	$\bar{0}$1200
	AM	TEST+11,5	00462	11	00437	$\bar{0}$0005
	AM	CALC+11,5	00474	11	00509	$\bar{0}$0005
	B	TEST	00486	49	00426	00000
CALC	M	HRSIN,RATE	00498	23	00604	00609
	.					
	.					
	.					
JOBIN	DC	2,0	00600	$\bar{0}$0		
HRSIN	DC	3,0	00602	$\bar{0}$00		
TAB	DC	2,01	00605	$\bar{0}$1		
RATE	DC	3,325	00607	$\bar{3}$25		

†See Figures 7-1 and 7-6.

	DC	2,02	00610 $\bar{0}2$
	DC	3,415	00612 $\bar{4}15$
	DC	2,04	00615 $\bar{0}4$
	DC	3,465	00617 $\bar{4}65$
	.		
	.		
	.		

2. 1620 SPS Using Indirect Addressing

	SYMBOLIC		*MACHINE LANGUAGE*			
	TFM	INDIR,TAB	00402	16	00599	$\bar{0}0606$
TEST	C	JOBIN,INDIR,11	00414	24	00601	$0059\bar{9}$
	BL	ERROR	00426	47	XXXXX	01300
	BE	CALC	00438	46	00474	01200
	AM	INDIR,5	00450	11	00599	$\bar{0}0005$
	B	TEST	00462	49	00414	00000
CALC	AM	INDIR,3	00474	11	00599	$\bar{0}0003$
	M	HRSIN,INDIR,11	00486	23	00604	$0059\bar{9}$
	.					
	.					
	.					
INDIR	DC	5,0	00595 $\bar{0}0000$			
JOBIN	DC	2,0	00600 $\bar{0}0$			
HRSIN	DC	3,0	00602 $\bar{0}00$			
TAB	DC	2,01	00605 $\bar{0}1$			
	DC	3,325	00607 $\bar{3}25$			
	DC	2,02	00610 $\bar{0}2$			
	DC	3,415	00612 $\bar{4}15$			
	.					
	.					
	.					

3. 360 Assembler Using a Table in Packed Format and a Base Register for Indexing

	PROGRAM		*COMMENTS*
	LA	7,TAB	Load the address of TAB into register 7
TEST	CP	JOBIN,0(2,7)	Compare JOBIN to contents of TAB
	BL	ERROR	
	BE	CALC	
	A	7,=F'4'	Increment Reg 7 by 4
	B	TEST	
CALC	MP	HRSIN,2(2,7)	A displacement of 2 bytes gives the appropriate rate
	.		
	.		
	.		

```
JOBIN   DC   PL2'0'
HRSIN   DC   PL4'0'
TAB     DC   P'01'      00 1C
        DC   P'325      32 5C
        DC   P'02'      00 2C
        DC   P'415'     41 5C
        .
        .
        .
```

Memory layout of table

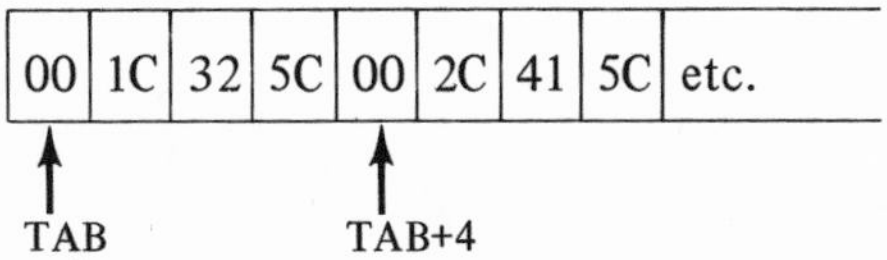

4. BASIC (assuming 20 entries in the table)

```
10   DIM T(20),R(20)
 .
 .
 .
40   FOR  I  =  1  TO20
50   IF  T(I)  =  J  THEN 80
60   NEXT I
70   STOP
80   LET  P  =  H*R(I)
 .
 .
 .
```

Definitions:

T = job number array
R = pay rate array
J = search job number
H = hours worked
P = gross pay

5. Fortran (assuming 20 entries in the table)

```
      DIMENSION  JOBTAB(20),  RATE(20)
       .
       .
       .
      DO  5  J  =  1,20,1
      IF (JOBTAB(J) - JOBIN) 5,6,7
5     CONTINUE
7     STOP
6     PAY  =  HRS * RATE (J)
       .
       .
       .
```

Appendix B

Program Documentation Time Card Extension

PROGRAM NUMBER 37

TIME CARD EXTENSION

DATE WRITTEN: NOVEMBER 1969 AUTHOR: J. PROGRAMMER

TABLE OF CONTENTS

PURPOSE OF THE PROGRAM

To prepare time card extension report from employee time cards containing card code (04), employee number, job number, and hours worked.

RECIPIENT OF REPORT: Payroll department
FREQUENCY OF REPORT: Weekly
AUTHORIZATION: Head of payroll department

CONTROLS

Cards are checked in the program for valid card code, sequence, and valid job number. The report of total hours is balanced to the hours in the control register. The total of the wages calculated is to be entered in the control register.

IBM GENERAL PURPOSE CARD PUNCHING FORM

JOB	*PAYROLL TIME CARDS*		
BY	*J. PROGRAMMER*	DATE	*NOV, 19XX*

PUNCHING INSTRUCTIONS

WRITTEN AS:											
PUNCH AS:											

NOTES:

FIELD IDENTIFICATION

1–2	3–7	8–9	10–12	13–80
CARD CODE	*EMPLOYEE NO.*	*JOB NO.*	*HOURS*	
04	XXXXX	XX	XX^X	← *UNUSED* →

CARD INPUT FORMAT

Printed in U.S.A. X20-8030-03 UM/025

PAGE *1* OF *1*

```
1                     TIME    CARD EXTENSION        PAGE XXX             [HEADING 1]
2
3         EMPLOYEE   HOURS      RATE                WAGE                 [HEADING 2]
4
5              XXXXX  XX.XCR      X.XX          XXX.XXCR                 [DETAIL LINE]
                         }          }               }
                   X,XXX.XCR*               XX,XXX.XXCR**                [TOTAL EMPLOYEE]

                   X,XXX.XCR*                                            [FINAL TOTAL]

               XXXXX                                  INVALID CARD CODE

               XXXXX                                  CARD OUT OF SEQUENCE - CANCEL JOB

                                                      JOB NO. NOT IN TABLE
               XXXXX
```

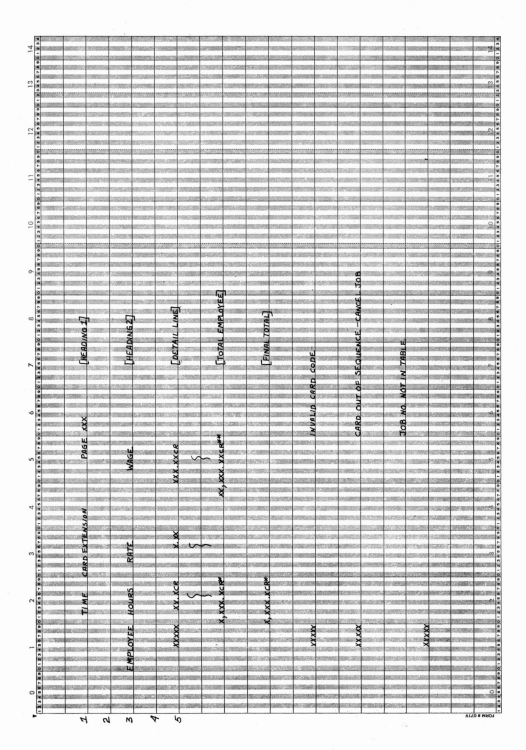

FORM # 071V

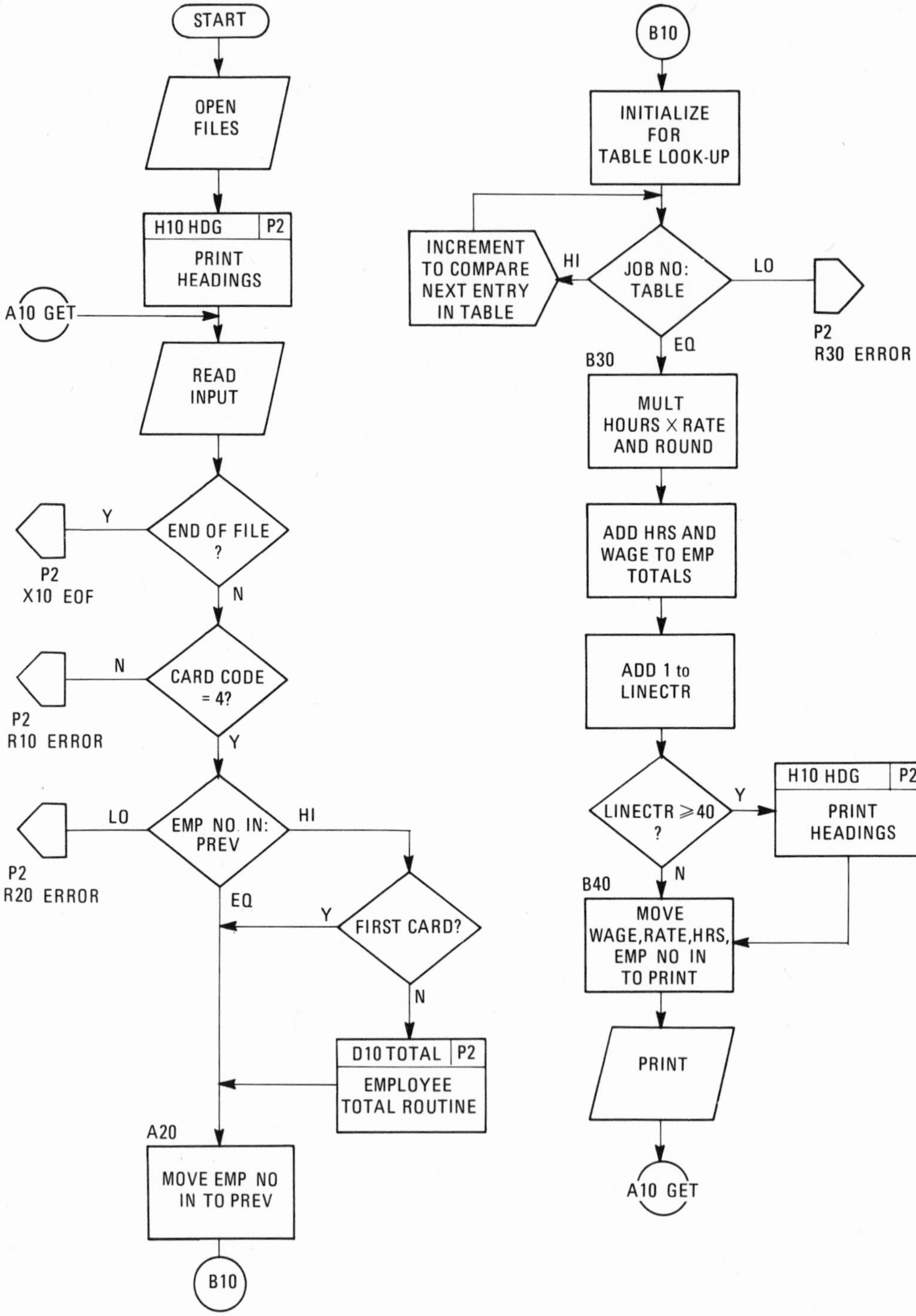
START
OPEN FILES
H10 HDG P2
PRINT HEADINGS
A10 GET
READ INPUT
END OF FILE ?
Y
P2 X10 EOF
N
CARD CODE = 4?
N
P2 R10 ERROR
Y
EMP NO. IN: PREV
LO
P2 R20 ERROR
HI
FIRST CARD?
Y
N
EQ
D10 TOTAL P2
EMPLOYEE TOTAL ROUTINE
A20
MOVE EMP NO IN TO PREV
B10
B10
INITIALIZE FOR TABLE LOOK-UP
INCREMENT TO COMPARE NEXT ENTRY IN TABLE
HI
JOB NO: TABLE
LO
P2 R30 ERROR
EQ
B30
MULT HOURS × RATE AND ROUND
ADD HRS AND WAGE TO EMP TOTALS
ADD 1 to LINECTR
LINECTR ≥40 ?
Y
H10 HDG P2
PRINT HEADINGS
N
B40
MOVE WAGE,RATE,HRS, EMP NO IN TO PRINT
PRINT
A10 GET

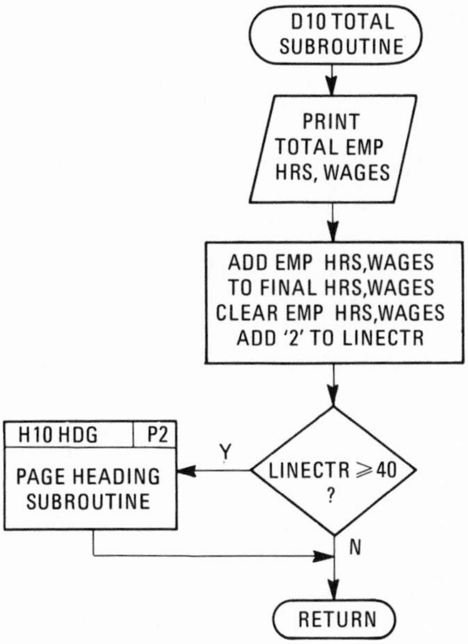

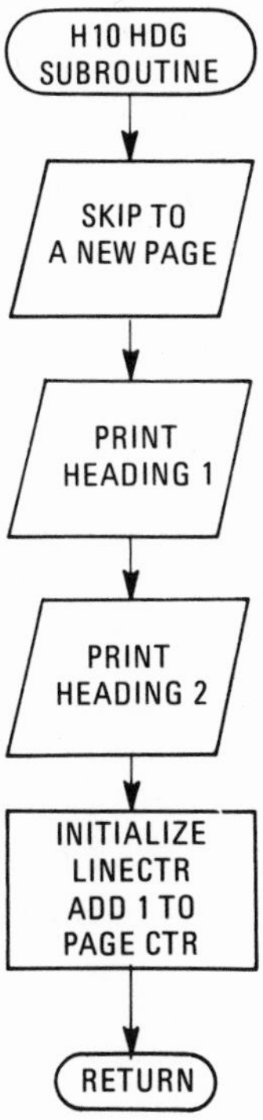

ERROR ROUTINES

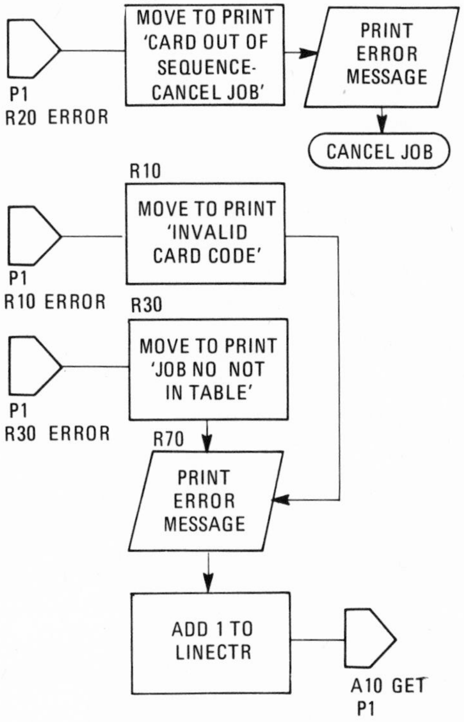

END OF FILE ROUTINE

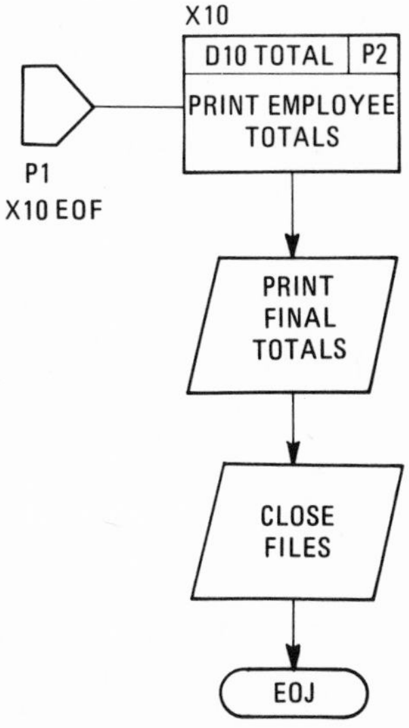

```
                                              PAYROLL TIME CARD EXTENSION                                         PAGE    2

  LOC  OBJECT CODE     ADDR1 ADDR2  STMT    SOURCE STATEMENT                                             DOS CL3-3 19/11/69

                                      2           PRINT ON,NODATA,NOGEN

002800                                4 PROGTLU   START X'2800'
002800 0540                           5 START     BALR  4,0                         INITIALIZE BASE REGISTER 4
002802                                6           USING *,4                         ESTAB. ADDRESSABILITY - 4K

                                      8           OPEN  CARD,PRTR                   ACTIVATE FILES
002816 4560 416C            0296E    17           BAL   6,H10HDG                    LINKAGE TO HEADING SUBROUTINE

                                     19 A10GET    GET   CARD,CARDIN                 READ A CARD
00282A D501 4488 462E 02C8A 02E30    25           CLC   CCODEIN,=C'04'              TEST FOR VALID CARD CODE
002830 4770 41DA            029DC    26           BNE   R10ERROR

002834 D504 448A 45AA 02C8C 02DAC    28           CLC   EMPNOIN,PREV                TEST FOR SEQUENCE
00283A 4780 404E            02850    29           BE    A20                              EQU - PROCESS CARD
00283E 4740 41E4            029E6    30           BL    R20ERROR                         LOW - ERROR
                                     31 *                                                 HI -
002842 D504 45AA 4634 02DAC 02E36    32           CLC   PREV,=CL5' '                TEST IF FIRST CARD OF FILE
002848 4780 404E            02850    33           BE    A20                              BRANCH TO PROCESS
00284C 4570 4100            02902    34           BAL   7,D10TOTAL                  NOT 1ST CARD LINK TO CTL BREAK
                                     35 *                                                SUBROUTINE
002850 D204 45AA 448A 02DAC 02C8C    36 A20       MVC   PREV,EMPNOIN                PROCESS CARD
002856 F212 45B1 4491 02DB3 02C93    37           PACK  HRSPK,HRSIN
00285C F211 45AF 448F 02DB1 02C91    38           PACK  JOBPK,JOBIN

                                     40 **              TABLE LOOK-UP FOR RATE OF PAY

002862 4190 45FA            02DFC    42 B10       LA    9,TAB                       LOAD ADDRESS OF TAB IN REG 9
002866 F911 45AF 9000 02DB1 00000    43 B20       CP    JOBPK,0(2,9)                COMPARE JOB NO TO TABLE
00286C 4740 420A            02A0C    44           BL    R30ERROR                    IF LOW,NOT IN TABLE - ERROR
002870 4780 407A            0287C    45           BE    B30
002874 4A90 4630            02E32    46           AH    9,=H'4'                     IF HIGH,INCREMENT REG 9 BY 4
002878 47F0 4064            02866    47           B     B20                              RETURN, TEST NEXT ENTRY

00287C F811 45B3 9002 02DB5 00002    49 B30       ZAP   RATEPK,2(2,9)               RATE DISPLACEMENT OF 2 BYTES
002882 F831 45B5 45B1 02DB7 02DB3    50           ZAP   WAGEPK,HRSPK
002888 FC31 45B5 45B3 02DB7 02DB5    51           MP    WAGEPK,RATEPK               HOURS TIMES RATE
00288E FA30 45B5 45B8 02DB7 02DBA    52           AP    WAGEPK,WAGEPK+3(1)          |0X|XX|.XX|XC|  ROUND
002894 F132 45B5 45B5 02DB7 02DB7    53           MVO   WAGEPK,WAGEPK(3)            |00|XX|X.X|XC| SHIFT RIGHT
00289A FA21 45B9 45B1 02DBB 02DB3    54           AP    EMPHRPK,HRSPK               ADD TOTAL HOURS & WAGES
0028A0 FA33 45BC 45B5 02DBE 02DB7    55           AP    EMPWGPK,WAGEPK                   FOR EMPLOYEE
0028A6 FA10 45C7 4639 02DC9 02E3B    56           AP    LINECTR,=P'1'               ADD TO LINE COUNTER
0028AC F911 45C7 4632 02DC9 02E34    57           CP    LINECTR,=P'40'              TEST IF EXCEEDS 40 LINES
0028B2 4740 40B8            028BA    58           BL    B40
0028B6 4560 416C            0296E    59           BAL   6,H10HDG                         IF YES GO TO HEAD ROUTINE

0028BA D208 4509 45CF 02D0B 02DD1    61 B40       MVC   PRINT+49(9),EDWD1           EDIT:
0028C0 DE08 4509 45B6 02D0B 02DB8    62           ED    PRINT+49(9),WAGEPK+1             WAGES
0028C6 D204 44FC 45D8 02CFE 02DDA    63           MVC   PRINT+36(5),EDWD2
0028CC DE04 44FC 45B3 02CFE 02DB5    64           ED    PRINT+36(5),RATEPK               RATE
0028D2 D206 44F0 45DD 02CF2 02DDF    65           MVC   PRINT+24(7),EDWD3
0028D8 DE06 44F0 45B1 02CF2 02DB3    66           ED    PRINT+24(7),HRSPK                HOURS
0028DE D204 44E7 448A 02CE9 02C8C    67           MVC   PRINT+15(5),EMPNOIN
0028E4 9209 44D8      02CDA          68           MVI   CTLCHAR,X'09'               SET UP PRINT  SPACE 1
                                     69           PUT   PRTR,PRINT                  PRINT
```

X

```
                                   PAYROLL TIME CARD EXTENSION                                        PAGE    3

  LOC  OBJECT CODE     ADDR1 ADDR2  STMT   SOURCE STATEMENT                                 DOS CL3-3 19/11/69

0028F8 D778 44D8 44D8 02CDA 02CDA    75             XC    PRINT,PRINT             CLEAR PRINT AREA
0028FE 47F0 4018            0281A    76             B     A10GET

                                     78 **        OUTPUT TOTAL HOURS & WAGES FOR EMPLOYEE - SUBROUTINE -

002902 D200 4512 4551 02D14 02D53    80 D10TOTAL MVC   PRINT+58(1),ASTERS
002908 D20B 4506 45E4 02D08 02DE6    81             MVC   PRINT+46(12),EDWD4      EDIT:
00290E DE0B 4506 45BC 02D08 02DBE    82             ED    PRINT+46(12),EMPWGPK        EMPLOYEE WAGES
002914 D200 44F7 4551 02CF9 02D53    83             MVC   PRINT+31(1),ASTERS
00291A D209 44ED 45F0 02CEF 02DF2    84             MVC   PRINT+21(10),EDWD5
002920 DE09 44ED 45B9 02CEF 02DBB    85             ED    PRINT+21(10),EMPHRPK        EMPLOYEE HOURS
002926 9211 44D8      02CDA          86             MVI   CTLCHAR,X'11'           SET UP PRINT,2 SPACES
                                     87             PUT   PRTR,PRINT
00293A D778 44D8 44D8 02CDA 02CDA    93             XC    PRINT,PRINT
002940 FA22 45C0 45B9 02DC2 02DBB    94             AP    TOTHRPK,EMPHRPK         ADD TO FINAL TOTAL HOURS
002946 FA33 45C3 45BC 02DC5 02DBE    95             AP    TOTWGPK,EMPWGPK             & WAGES
00294C F820 45B9 463A 02DBB 02E3C    96             ZAP   EMPHRPK,=P'0'           CLEAR EMPLOYEE HOURS
002952 F830 45BC 463A 02DBE 02E3C    97             ZAP   EMPWGPK,=P'0'               & WAGES
002958 FA10 45C7 463B 02DC9 02E3D    98             AP    LINECTR,=P'2'           ADD TO LINE COUNTER
00295E F911 45C7 4632 02DC9 02E34    99             CP    LINECTR,=P'40'          TEST IF EXCEEDS 40 LINES
002964 4740 416A            0296C   100             BL    D20
002968 4560 416C            0296E   101             BAL   6,H10HDG
00296C 07F7                         102 D20         BR    7                       BRANCH TO ADDR REG7-A20 OR X20

                                    104 **          PAGE HEADING SUB-ROUTINE

00296E 928B 44D8      02CDA         106 H10HDG      MVI   CTLCHAR,X'8B'           SKIP TO A
                                    107             PUT   PRTR,PRINT                  NEW PAGE
002982 D203 451B 45CB 02D1D 02DCD   113             MVC   PRINT+67(4),EDPAGE      EDIT
002988 DE03 451B 45C9 02D1D 02DCB   114             ED    PRINT+67(4),PAGECTR         PAGE COUNTER
00298E D22B 44EE 4553 02CF0 02D55   115             MVC   PRINT+22(44),HDG1
002994 9211 44D8      02CDA         116             MVI   CTLCHAR,X'11'
                                    117             PUT   PRTR,PRINT              PRINT FIRST LINE HEADING
0029A8 D778 44D8 44D8 02CDA 02CDA   123             XC    PRINT,PRINT
0029AE D22A 44E5 457F 02CE7 02D81   124             MVC   PRINT+13(43),HDG2       PRINT SECOND LINE HEADING
0029B4 9211 44D8      02CDA         125             MVI   CTLCHAR,X'11'
                                    126             PUT   PRTR,PRINT
0029C8 D778 44D8 44D8 02CDA 02CDA   132             XC    PRINT,PRINT
0029CE F810 45C7 463C 02DC9 02E3E   133             ZAP   LINECTR,=P'5'           INITIALIZE LINE COUNT TO LINE5
0029D4 FA10 45C9 4639 02DCB 02E3B   134             AP    PAGECTR,=P'1'           ADD TO PAGE COUNTER
0029DA 07F6                         135             BR    6                       RETURN LINKAGE

                                    137 **          ERROR  ROUTINE

0029DC D210 4514 463D 02D16 02E3F   139 R10ERROR MVC   PRINT+60(17),=C'INVALID CARD CODE'
0029E2 47F0 4210            02A12   140             B     R70

0029E6 D21E 4514 464E 02D16 02E50   142 R20ERROR MVC   PRINT+60(31),=C'CARD OUT OF SEQUENCE-CANCEL JOB'
0029EC D204 44E7 448A 02CE9 02C8C   143             MVC   PRINT+15(5),EMPNOIN
0029F2 9209 44D8      02CDA         144             MVI   CTLCHAR,X'09'
                                    145             PUT   PRTR,PRINT              PRINT ERROR MESSAGE
                                    151             CANCEL ALL                    CANCEL THE JOB

002A0C D212 4514 466D 02D16 02E6F   156 R30ERROR MVC   PRINT+60(19),=C'JOB NO.NOT IN TABLE'
```

```
  LOC  OBJECT CODE     ADDR1 ADDR2  STMT   SOURCE STATEMENT                                          DOS CL3-3 19/11/69

002A12 D204 44E7 448A 02CE9 02C8C   158 R70        MVC   PRINT+15(5),EMPNOIN
002A18 9209 44D8      02CDA         159            MVI   CTLCHAR,X'09'
                                    160            PUT   PRTR,PRINT              PRINT ERROR MESSAGE
002A2C D778 44D8 44D8 02CDA 02CDA   166            XC    PRINT,PRINT
002A32 FA10 45C7 4639 02DC9 02E3B   167            AP    LINECTR,=P'1'
002A38 47F0 4018            0281A   168            B     A10GET

                                    170 **         END  OF FILE ROUTINE

002A3C 4570 4100            02902   172 X10EOF     BAL   7,D10TOTAL              LINK TO PRINT LAST EMPLOYEE
002A40 D201 4512 4551 02D14 02D53   173 X20        MVC   PRINT+58(2),ASTERS
002A46 D20B 4506 45E4 02D08 02DE6   174            MVC   PRINT+46(12),EDWD4      EDIT:
002A4C DE0B 4506 45C3 02D08 02DC5   175            ED    PRINT+46(12),TOTWGPK        TOTAL WAGES
002A52 D201 44F7 4551 02CF9 02D53   176            MVC   PRINT+31(2),ASTERS
002A58 D209 44ED 45F0 02CEF 02DF2   177            MVC   PRINT+21(10),EDWD5
002A5E DE09 44ED 45C0 02CEF 02DC2   178            ED    PRINT+21(10),TOTHRPK        TOTAL HOURS
002A64 9209 44D8      02CDA         179            MVI   CTLCHAR,X'09'           SET UP SPACE 1
                                    180            PUT   PRTR,PRINT              PRINT FINAL TOTALS
                                    186            CLOSE CARD,PRTR               DE-ACTIVATE FILES
                                    195            EOJ

                                    199 **         D E C L A R A T I V E S

                                    201 CARD       DTFCD BLKSIZE=80,             DEFINE THE CARD FILE       C
                                                         DEVADDR=SYSIPT,                                    C
                                                         DEVICE=2501,                                       C
                                                         EOFADDR=X10EOF,                                    C
                                                         IOAREA1=IOARCAR1,                                  C
                                                         IOAREA2=IOARCAR2,                                  C
                                                         TYPEFLE=INPUT,                                     C
                                                         WORKA=YES

                                    222 PRTR       DTFPR BLKSIZE=121,            DEFINE THE PRINTER FILE    C
                                                         CTLCHR=YES,                                        C
                                                         DEVADDR=SYSLST,                                    C
                                                         DEVICE=1443,                                       C
                                                         IOAREA1=IOARPRT1,                                  C
                                                         IOAREA2=IOARPRT2,                                  C
                                                         WORKA=YES

002AF8                              244 IOARCAR1 DS      CL80                    BUFFER-1 CARD FILE
002B48                              245 IOARCAR2 DS      CL80                    BUFFER-2 CARD FILE
002B98                              246 IOARPRT1 DS      CL121                   BUFFER-1 PRINTER FILE
002C11                              247 IOARPRT2 DS      CL121                   BUFFER-2 PRINTER FILE

002C8A                              249 CARDIN   DS      0CL80                   CARD INPUT AREA
002C8A                              250 CCODEIN  DS      CL2
002C8C                              251 EMPNOIN  DS      CL5
002C91                              252 JOBIN    DS      CL2
002C93                              253 HRSIN    DS      CL3          (XX.X)
002C96                              254          DS      CL68

002CDA                              256 CTLCHAR  DS      0CL1                    PRINTER
002CDA 4040404040404040             257 PRINT    DC      CL121'                      OUTPUT AREA
                                    258 *
```

```
                                          PAYROLL TIME CARD EXTENSION                                       PAGE    5

  LOC  OBJECT CODE     ADDR1 ADDR2  STMT   SOURCE STATEMENT                                        DOS CL3-3 19/11/69

002D53 5C5C                          260 ASTERS    DC     C'**'
002D55 E340C940D440C540              261 HDG1      DC     C'T I M E  C A R D  E X T E N S I O N    PAGE'
002D81 C5D4D7D3D6E8C5C5              262 HDG2      DC     C'EMPLOYEE   HOURS          RATE           WAGE'
002DAC 4040404040                    263 PREV      DC     CL5' '

002DB1 000C                          265 JOBPK     DC     PL2'0'
002DB3 000C                          266 HRSPK     DC     PL2'0'                |XX|.XC|
002DB5 000C                          267 RATEPK    DC     PL2'0'                |X.X|XC|
002DB7 0000000C                      268 WAGEPK    DC     PL4'0'
002DBB 00000C                        269 EMPHRPK   DC     PL3'0'
002DBE 0000000C                      270 EMPWGPK   DC     PL4'0'
002DC2 00000C                        271 TOTHRPK   DC     PL3'0'
002DC5 0000000C                      272 TOTWGPK   DC     PL4'0'
002DC9 000C                          273 LINECTR   DC     PL2'0'
002DCB 001C                          274 PAGECTR   DC     PL2'1'

002DCD 40202020                      276 EDPAGE    DC     X'40202020'
002DD1 402020214B2020C3              277 EDWD1     DC     X'402020214B2020C3D9'
002DDA 40204B2020                    278 EDWD2     DC     X'40204B2020'
002DDF 4020214B20C3D9                279 EDWD3     DC     X'4020214B20C3D9'
002DE6 4020206B2020214B              280 EDWD4     DC     X'4020206B2020214B2020C3D9'
002DF2 40206B2020214B20              281 EDWD5     DC     X'40206B2020214B20C3D9'

                                     283 **                TABLE OF JOB NOS. & RATES  ( INCOMPLETE )

002DFC 001C                          285 TAB       DC     P'01'                 |00|1C|  2 BYTES JOB NO.
002DFE 325C                          286           DC     P'3.25'               |32|.5C| 2 BYTES RATE
002E00 002C                          287           DC     P'02'
002E02 415C                          288           DC     P'4.15'
002E04 004C                          289           DC     P'04'
002E06 345C                          290           DC     P'3.45'
002E08 099C                          291           DC     P'99'
002E0A 350C                          292           DC     P'3.50'

002E10                               294           LTORG
002E10 5B5BC2D6D7C5D540              295                  =C'$$BOPEN '
002E18 5B5BC2C3D3D6E2C5              296                  =C'$$BCLOSE'
002E20 00002A90                      297                  =A(CARD)
002E24 00002C8A                      298                  =A(CARDIN)
002E28 00002AC8                      299                  =A(PRTR)
002E2C 00002CDA                      300                  =A(PRINT)
002E30 F0F4                          301                  =C'04'
002E32 0004                          302                  =H'4'
002E34 040C                          303                  =P'40'
002E36 4040404040                    304                  =CL5' '
002E3B 1C                            305                  =P'1'
002E3C 0C                            306                  =P'0'
002E3D 2C                            307                  =P'2'
002E3E 5C                            308                  =P'5'
002E3F C9D5E5C1D3C9C440              309                  =C'INVALID CARD CODE'
002E50 C3C1D9C440D6E4E3              310                  =C'CARD OUT OF SEQUENCE-CANCEL JOB'
002E6F D1D6C240D5D64BD5              311                  =C'JOB NO.NOT IN TABLE'
002800                               312           END    START
```

DESCRIPTION

Cards are in sequence by employee number. The rate of pay for each job is stored in a table in the program. The job number on each time card is used to locate the correct rate of pay from the table. The wage for each time card is calculated by multiplying hours and rate and is printed. Total hours and wages by employee and for final total are printed.

The program is organized into the following sections:

A = reading cards and sequence checking
B = table look-up
D = employee total subroutine
H = page heading subroutine
R = error routines
X = end of job routine

SPECIAL FEATURES

Example of multiply calculation:

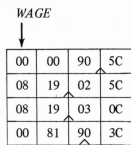

	WAGE ↓			
Store Hrs (90.5) in WAGE	00	00	90	5C
Multiply by RATE (9.05)	08	19	02	5C
Half-adjust	08	19	03	0C
Shift right one digit	00	81	90	3C

TABLE FORMAT

4 BYTES							
2 BYTES		2 BYTES					
00	1C	32	5C	00	2C	41	5C
Job 1		Rate 1		Job 2		Rate 2	
1st ENTRY				2nd ENTRY			

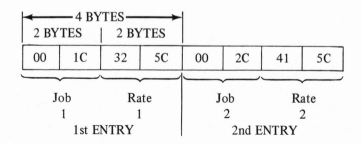

All fields are in packed format:

Argument:	Job number	2 bytes	
Function:	Rate	2 bytes	(X.XX)
		4 bytes	

REGISTER USAGE

4 Base register for first 4096 bytes
6 Linkage register for page heading subroutine
7 Linkage register for employee total subroutine
9 Register for indexing table look-up

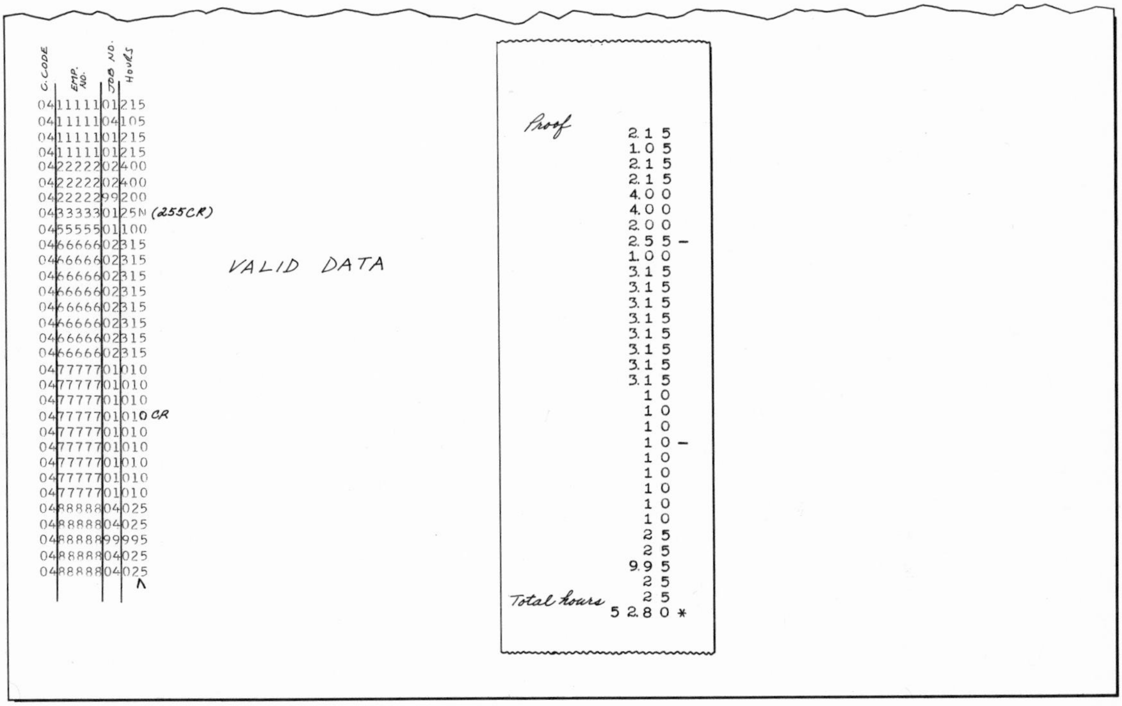
C.CODE
EMP. NO.
JOB NO.
HOURS
04111110121
04111110410
04111110121
04111110121
04222220240
04222220240
04222229920
04333330125N (255CR)
04555550110
04666660231
04666660231
04666660231
04666660231
04666660231
04666660231
04666660231
04666660231
04777770101
04777770101
04777770101
04777770101 0 CR
04777770101
04777770101
04777770101
04777770101
04777770101
04888880402
04888880402
04888889999
04888880402
04888880402
VALID DATA
Proof
2.15
1.05
2.15
2.15
4.00
4.00
2.00
2.55 -
1.00
3.15
3.15
3.15
3.15
3.15
3.15
3.15
3.15
10
10
10
10 -
10
10
10
10
10
25
25
9.95
25
25
Total hours
52.80 *

TIME CARD EXTENSION PAGE 1

EMPLOYEE	HOURS	RATE	WAGE
11111	21.5	3.25	69.88
11111	10.5	3.45	36.23
11111	21.5	3.25	69.88
11111	21.5	3.25	69.88
	75.0 *		245.87 *
22222	40.0	4.15	166.00
22222	40.0	4.15	166.00
22222	20.0	3.50	70.00
	100.0 *		402.00 *
33333	25.5CR	3.25	82.88CR
	25.5CR*		82.88CR*
55555	10.0	3.25	32.50
	10.0 *		32.50 *
66666	31.5	4.15	130.73
66666	31.5	4.15	130.73
66666	31.5	4.15	130.73
66666	31.5	4.15	130.73
66666	31.5	4.15	130.73
66666	31.5	4.15	130.73
66666	31.5	4.15	130.73
66666	31.5	4.15	130.73
	252.0 *		1,045.84 *
77777	1.0	3.25	3.25
77777	1.0	3.25	3.25
77777	1.0	3.25	3.25
77777	1.0CR	3.25	3.25CR
77777	1.0	3.25	3.25
77777	1.0	3.25	3.25
77777	1.0	3.25	3.25

OUTPUT

VALID DATA

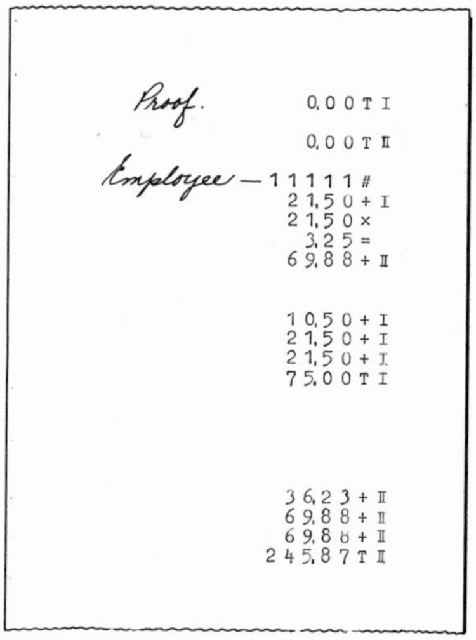

```
            T I M E   C A R D   E X T E N S I O N      PAGE    2

EMPLOYEE    HOURS         RATE          WAGE

  77777       1.0         3.25           3.25
  77777       1.0         3.25           3.25
              7.0  *                    22.75  *

  88888       2.5         3.45           8.63
  88888       2.5         3.45           8.63
  88888      99.5         3.50         348.25
  88888       2.5         3.45           8.63
  88888       2.5         3.45           8.63
            109.5  *                   382.77  *

            528.0  **                2,048.85  **
```

VALID DATA (cont.)

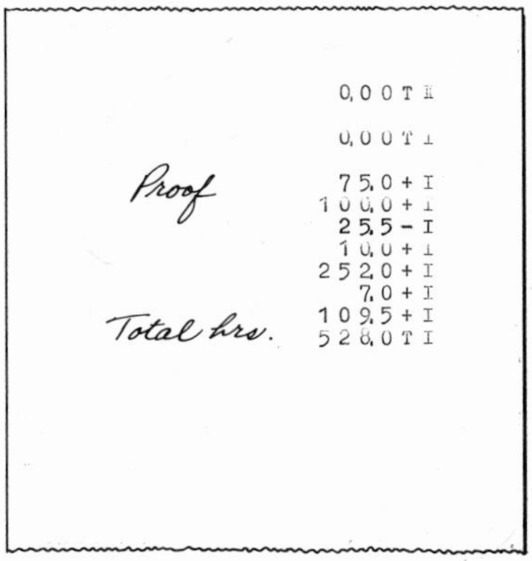

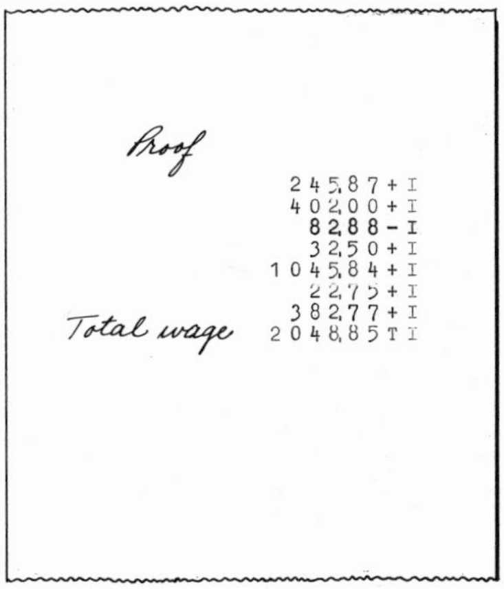

C CODE	EMP NO.	JOB NO	HRS
04	11111	01	215
04	11111	04	105
04	11111	01	215
04	11111	01	215
04	22222	02	400
04	22222	03	200
04	22222	02	400
04	22222	99	200
04	22222	98	200
04	55555	01	100
55	55555	01	100
04	11111	04	105
04	66666	02	315
04	66666	02	315

INVALID DATA

T I M E C A R D E X T E N S I O N   PAGE 1

EMPLOYEE	HOURS		RATE	WAGE		
11111	21.5		3.25	69.88		
11111	10.5		3.45	36.23		
11111	21.5		3.25	69.88		
11111	21.5		3.25	69.88		
	75.0	*		245.87	*	
22222	40.0		4.15	166.00		
22222						JOB NO.NOT IN TABLE
22222	40.0		4.15	166.00		
22222	20.0		3.50	70.00		
22222						JOB NO.NOT IN TABLE
	100.0	*		402.00	*	
55555	10.0		3.25	32.50		
55555						INVALID CARD CODE
11111						CARD OUT OF SEQUENCE-CANCEL JOB

INVALID DATA

OPERATION SECTION

Input: Card file payroll time cards, card code 04, in employee number sequence. Run weekly.

Output: Printed report "TIME CARD EXTENSION." Form required: stock tab, two-part, 14 X 11 inches. Standard carriage control tape.

CORE SIZE	*HEX.*	*DEC.*	
Hi	X'2F75'	12,149	
Lo	X'2800'	10,240	
		1,909	Bytes

Job control cards: Not included with this example.

Restrictions: Field sizes:

PAGECTR = 999 pages
LINECTR = 40 lines

	TIME CARD	*EMPLOYEE TOTAL*	*FINAL TOTAL*
Hours	99.9	9,999.9	9,999.9
Wages ($)	9.99	99,999.99	99,999.99

Employee total hours are not expected to exceed 999.9 and wages 9999.99, but are extra large to facilitate editing.

ERROR ROUTINES

MESSAGE AND PROGRAM LABEL

INVALID CARD CODE: (R10ERROR)	Card code is not 04. Card is not processed. Job continues.
CARD OUT OF SEQUENCE: (R20ERROR)	Cards are not in ascending sequence by employee number. Job is canceled. Cards must be checked and sorted and job rerun.
JOB NO. NOT IN TABLE: (R30ERROR)	Card contains unlisted job number. Card is not processed. Job continues.

Appendix C

Translators

BACKGROUND

On the early computers the programmer had to code the instructions in *machine language.* He had to assign all the memory addresses of instructions, constants, and counters and had to reference them by these addresses. Appendix A, Example 1, shows machine language on the right side.

This practice was time-consuming and subject to many coding errors. *Symbolic languages* were devised to overcome these problems. The instruction codes were given symbolic names. For example, the symbol for a branch instruction, 49, became a B. Constants could be given symbolic labels. The program could then be written in symbolic language as shown in the same example on the left side. The computer, however, is unable to execute symbolic code. The manufacturer supplies a *translator program* such as Assembler and Cobol that will translate the symbolic code into machine language.

PROCEDURE FOR TRANSLATING

The programmer writes, for example, a payroll program in symbolic language on a specially designed coding sheet. The coding is then keypunched into cards, usually one card for each line of coding. This produces the program *source deck.*

The translator program is loaded from cards, tape, or disk into the computer memory. The source deck is read as data to the translator. The translator assigns addresses to the instructions and the constants and produces a machine language executable *object program.* In addition, it produces a diagnostic report of all the errors it is able to find, such as invalid symbolic instructions and undefined constants. On receiving the object listing, the programmer must correct all these errors and re-submit the source deck for translating. Even when there are no errors reported, however, there may still be program errors; the translator cannot find errors in logic.

The translator program then permanently records the object program on cards, tape, or disk. When it is required to process the payroll program, the operator loads the payroll object program into memory from the cards, tape, or disk, and then enters the payroll data to be processed.

TYPES OF TRANSLATORS

There are two main types of translators, the low-level assembler and the high-level compiler.

1. *Assemblers.* Examples are 1620 SPS, 1401 Autocoder, Honeywell Easycoder, 360 Assembler. Generally these are translated so that one source statement produces one object machine instruction. These languages are machine-dependent and machine-oriented. Normally the assembler language is unique to the particular computer and its characteristics. A 1620 SPS program, for example, will not run on any other computer. When the data processing department replaces the computer with a newer model or one from a different manufacturer, the programs must be rewritten.
2. *Compilers.* Examples are Algol, Basic, Cobol, Fortran and PL/I. Unlike assemblers, they are translated so that one source statement often generates many machine instructions.

> Compiler languages are more machine-independent and problem-oriented. The compiler source language may be translated by many computers. For example, Burroughs, Honeywell, IBM, and Univac have Cobol compilers.

The advantages of compilers are, first, they are much easier to write. Involved arithmetic calculations, which are difficult to write in assembler language, are simple in compiler language. Second, they are easier to read and, therefore, easier to amend. Third, they are more adaptable for use on different computers. Although the source program must be re-compiled, it need not be rewritten.

The disadvantages of compilers are, first, that they tend to produce more machine instructions than an assembler program does. Therefore, they require more memory for the program and more time to execute. Second, they are less capable than assemblers in accessing parts of fields or single memory positions.

Which type of translator will be used will depend on the following factors:

Computer memory size
Availability of translator
Experience of the staff
Future plans of the department.

Index

POWWOW

Festivals and Holidays

By June Behrens

Photographs compiled by Terry Behrens

CHILDRENS PRESS, CHICAGO

TO BLANCHE BREWSTER

ACKNOWLEDGMENTS

The author wishes to acknowledge with thanks the assistance of Eva Northrup, called Seyweemana, of the Hopi Indian tribe. Ms. Northrup serves as project manager of EONA, Educational Opportunities for Native Americans, in the Long Beach Unified School District, Long Beach, California. A special thanks to Dan James of the Choctaw tribe, teacher in the Long Beach Unified School District.

PHOTO CREDITS

David Tuch: COVER photograph
Selected scenes
Elyn Marton: Selected scenes

Library of Congress Cataloging in Publication Data

Behrens, June.
Powwow.

(Festivals and holidays)
Summary: Describes a visit to a powwow, or Native American celebration, where American Indian families get together to enjoy traditional food, music, dancing, and crafts.
1. Indians of North America—Rites and ceremonies—Juvenile literature.
[1. Indians of North America—Rites and ceremonies. 2. Festivals] I. Behrens, Terry, ill. II. Title. III. Series.
E98.R3B285 1983 394.2'68'08997 83-7274
ISBN 0-516-02387-X

5 6 7 8 9 10 11 R 93 92

Listen to the drums! They are the heartbeat of the Powwow. The dancers move faster and faster. They keep perfect time with the beat of the drums.

Our friend Red Elk has invited us to the Powwow. In school, Red Elk is called Billy.

The Powwow is a special gathering for Native American families. Native Americans are descendants of Indians who lived in America before the early settlers came.

Red Elk tells us the Powwow is an American Indian ceremony and tribal custom. Sometimes it is called a Tribal Fair or an Indian Days Festival. It might celebrate a special date, or just be a time to get together for fun. Powwow is a grand picnic with food and singing and drums and dancing!

The Powwow pulls tribes and families together. It brings pride and harmony into their hearts. At the Powwow the elders pass on the old ways, or traditions, to the young. Indian dancers follow in the steps of their ancestors. The songs have been sung by many generations.

Skills at games and storytelling are passed from parents to children, as are tribal arts and crafts.

Red Elk takes us to see his uncle, Good Eagle, the pipe maker. Good Eagle greets us with *hau, wakanyeja.* This means "Hello, children" in the Sioux language.

Good Eagle tells us the Powwow may be small, with just a few families. Or, it could be a large gathering, with thousands of people coming from many tribes and many states. Those who come from far away bring campers and vans. Sometimes they may even pitch their teepees!

At the Powwow the Native Americans might speak English or the language of their tribe. There are many tribes and many languages.

Good Eagle says the contests are an important part of the Powwow. Who will be chosen the best dancers and singers? Everyone wants to know.

The fancy dancers wear beautiful costumes of feathers and beads. They paint their faces and bodies. The designs might be passed down from one generation to another. Dancers spend hours getting ready for contests.

This Powwow will last for one day. Others might last for four or five days. Many Powwows are held each year in various parts of the United States.

This Powwow is in a park. Some Powwows are held on fairgrounds and farms or on Indian reservations. Often a rodeo and crafts fair are part of the Powwow.

Red Elk wants us to try the fry bread. It's his favorite. Fry bread looks like a large pancake sprinkled with powdered sugar. Is it good!

Red Elk reminds us that Native Americans have given us many gifts of food. Long ago they cultivated wild plants. Today we enjoy corn, potatoes, beans, tomatoes, and many other foods first grown by Indian farmers long ago. We can thank them for popcorn, peanuts, and chewing gum, too.

Red Elk shows us a sand painting. We watch the artist sprinkle colored sand into the design. The design may be a god or a sacred symbol used many times before.

Red Elk says that once sand painting was used by the elders for healing. If someone were ill, a sand painting was made in a day and destroyed before sunset. Many people believed the sand took away the cause of the illness.

Look at the beautiful beads and jewelry! Red Elk tells us that Indians know which tribe made the jewelry by the patterns in the work. Native American jewelry is made from seeds, bones, feathers, and shells. Stones, such as turquoise and coral, are set in silver by skilled silversmiths.

Making baskets, rugs, and blankets are weaving skills passed from mother to daughter. The elders are eager for the young people to carry on their work as artists.

What is the game those children are playing? It's called "hunt the stones." We run all over the park to find the stones!

Red Elk shows us how to play a guessing game. He has a bone hidden in each hand. One bone is plain and the other is marked. We must try to guess which hand holds the unmarked bone.

These are the same games played by Indian children long ago.

Red Elk tells us about the Kachina doll. It represents Kachina spirits, or supernatural beings. They are the mythical ancestors of the Pueblo people. Kachina spirits might bring plentiful crops or gifts for the children.

Indians believed in the spirit forces in nature. They believed animals and plants, as well as the sun, wind, and rain, had spirits just like people. Disasters were caused by evil or angered spirits.

Miracle workers, called medicine men, were supposed to have power to influence spirit forces. Many modern Indians still practice these beliefs.

We know that Red Elk's ancestors were the first people in America. They explored and cultivated the land long before the settlers came from Europe.

In each region of America there were many tribes and many cultures. The woodland Indians lived in the eastern forests. The plains Indians were the hunters, and roamed over the Midwest's grassy plains.

The shepherds of the Southwest herded animals, and the farmers planted crops. The seed gatherers of the West were wanderers, and the Northwest Indians were fishermen. Red Elk and his family are from the Sioux tribe. In early times his people were plains Indians.

As our nation grew, the settlers moved to new places. The land where Indians had lived was taken by white men. Many Indians were sent from their homes to Indian Territory. The lands reserved for Indians became reservations. Reservations were public lands set aside by the United States government as homes for Native Americans.

Good Eagle tells us that in 1924 Native Americans were made citizens. Many are citizens of their Indian nation tribes as well as United States citizens.

There are about 1.5 million Indians in the United States. Over half of them no longer live on reservations. They live in cities and towns in all parts of America.

California is called the Indian capital because this state has the most Indians living in it. More than 200,000 Indians from many tribes live in California.

Red Elk and his family often go to the Indian Center. Here they can meet their friends and keep alive respect and pride for the old ways of the elders. The Indian Center helps to organize Powwows and brings people together from all the tribes.

Here come the dancers again! Listen to the music. Drums and rattles, whistles and flutes are the music makers. They make the rhythm for the singers and dancers.

These dances are for fun and show. Let's see who is best. All ages dance, from the very young to the skilled men's fancy dancers.

Each dance has a meaning. Some dancers imitate animal and bird movements. Others tell stories of events in the lives of the people.

Long ago, dances were for religious or magical reasons, too. Indians danced to heal the sick, to bring rain, or to make the corn grow. There were special dances for the buffalo hunt. Other dances told the history of the tribe. Sometimes the costumes help us to understand what the dance is about.

We thank Red Elk and Good Eagle for sharing their Powwow. We have eaten fry bread and watched the craftsmen. We have heard the drums and swayed with the painted dancers. We have listened to the singers and played the games. We have become a part of the Powwow spirit.

We say *ake wancinyankin kte.* In the Sioux language this means "We'll see you again, at the next Powwow!"

Epilogue

All life that is holy and good for we two-leggeds
is shared with the four-leggeds
and the wings of the air
and all green things; for these are children
of one mother
and their father is one spirit.

Black Elk

Powwow is a social gathering for Native Americans. It pulls tribes and extended families together and unites them in a revival of Indian pride.

Powwow reflects one aspect of Indian life as it is today, within the framework of ceremonies and traditions, music and dance, arts and crafts.

We glimpse the history of a people and learn about their early beliefs and cultural contributions. We are brought into scenes that capture the spirit of Powwow and bring us to a better understanding of our Native American friends and neighbors.

Powwow gives us a feeling for the underlying thread of the old and the new in today's society.

JUNE BEHRENS has written more than fifty books, plays, and filmstrips for young people, touching on all subject areas of the school curriculum. *Powwow* is the third book in the Festivals and Holidays Series. Mrs. Behrens has for many years been an educator in one of California's largest public school systems. She is a graduate of the University of California at Santa Barbara and has a Master's degree from the University of Southern California. Mrs. Behrens is listed in *Who's Who of American Women.* She is a recipient of the Distinguished Alumni Award from the University of California for her contributions in the field of education. She and her husband live in Rancho Palos Verdes, a Southern California suburb.

TERRY BEHRENS has compiled the photographs for three books in the Festivals and Holidays Series. Ms. Behrens is a photographer and a teacher of English as a Second Language in the California public schools. She is a graduate of California Polytechnic University and has studied at the University of London and Universidad de Morelos in Mexico.

DAVID TUCH is a retired businessman, philanthropist, and professional photographer. His work as a photographer has won international acclaim. A one man show in Hong Kong earned him a life membership in the Chinese Photographic Society. His photography has been featured in *Westways, People's Almanac,* and other prominent publications. His work was displayed in the Fine Arts Pavillion of the 1982 World's Fair, and is on permanent exhibit at Skirball Museum in Los Angeles.